If These Walls Could Speak

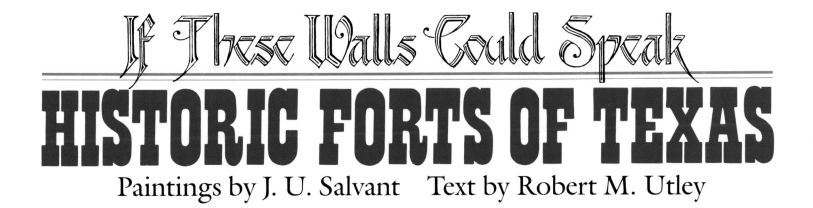

HISTORIC FORTS OF TEXAS

Paintings by J. U. Salvant   Text by Robert M. Utley

UNIVERSITY OF TEXAS PRESS — AUSTIN

Copyright © 1985 by the University of Texas Press
All rights reserved
Printed in Japan

First paperback printing, 1990

Requests for permission
to reproduce material from this work
should be sent to: Permissions
University of Texas Press,
Box 7819, Austin, Texas 78713-7819

∞ The paper used in this publication meets the
minimum requirements of American National
Standard for Information Sciences—Permanence of
Paper for Printed Library Materials, ANSI Z39.48-1984.

Publication of this book was assisted by
funds from Muse Air Corporation.

LIBRARY OF CONGRESS
CATALOGING-IN-PUBLICATION DATA

Salvant, J. U. (Joan Usner), 1932–
    If these walls could speak.
    Bibliography: p.
    1. Salvant, J. U. (Joan Usner), 1932–
2. Fortifications in art. 3. Fortifications—Texas—
History.
I. Utley, Robert Marshall, 1929–
II. Title.
ND237.C263A4   1985   759.13   85-9127
ISBN 0-292-73865-X pbk.

CONTENTS

To my husband, EDWIN THEODORE SALVANT, JR.,
for his love, patience, support, and constructive criticism,

to my father, CLARENCE LEONARD USNER,
for sharing his knowledge of history and architecture with me,

and to my dear friend, MARY ANNE KELLEY MCCLOUD, for her faith and vision,

this book is dedicated.

J.U.S.

ACKNOWLEDGMENTS

Information on the forts and their history was provided by the following people and institutions: Douglas McChristian and Mary L. Williams, Fort Davis National Historical Site, Fort Davis; Margaret Blanco, Fort Bliss Replica Museum, El Paso; Jay A. Matthews, Jr., B.G., Texas ARNG (Retired), Military History Associates of Texas and the Southwest, Austin; John F. Vaughan, Director, and Robert F. Bluthardt, Educational Director, Fort Concho Museum, San Angelo; Texas Parks and Wildlife Library, Austin, where I found journals on excavation and historical research for Forts Griffin, Lancaster, McKavett, and Richardson; National Archives, Washington, D.C., where I consulted architectural documents for Forts Brown, McIntosh, Ringgold, Davis, and Bliss; Nuevo Santander Museum, Laredo; and Panhandle-Plains Museum, Canyon.

Further information was obtained from the following books and articles: *I Married a Soldier* (diary), by Lydia Spencer Lane (Albuquerque: Horn Wallace Publisher, Inc., 1964); *Forts of the West* by Robert W. Frazer (Norman: University of Oklahoma Press, 1965); *American Artillery in the Mexican War, 1846–47* by Lester R. Dillon (Austin: Presidial Press, 1975); *Artillery through the Ages* by Albert Manucy (Washington, D.C.: U.S. Government Printing Office, 1977); "A Black Lieutenant in the Ranks," by Steve Wilson, *American History* 18, no. 8 (December 1983); "Courtmartial of Lt. Henry O. Flipper," by Bruce J. Dinges, *The American West* 9, no. 1 (January 1972); *Flipper's Dismissal* by Barry C. Johnson (London, 1980); and two articles available in micrographed form at Fort Davis: "Theoretical Wardrobe of Alice Kirk Grierson" by Mary Williams, and "Theoretical Wardrobe of Colonel B. H. Grierson" by Douglas McChristian.

The following have been of considerable assistance in the creation of this book: Mr. and Mrs. Austin McCloud, Mr. and Mrs. Henry Musselman, Mr. and Mrs. Johnny Musselman, Mr. and Mrs. David Burgher, Mr. and Mrs. C. A. Wilkins, Mr. and Mrs. Michael Muse, Ms. Janet Parker, Mr. and Mrs. Joseph Ethridge, Mr. Byron Price, Mr. and Mrs. Ted Williford, Dr. and Mrs. H. J. Bulgerin, Mr. and Mrs. John Iman, Col. (Ret.) and Mrs. Verne D. J. Philips, Mr. and Mrs. Manuel B. Bravo, Jr., Mr. William Griggs, Dr. Douglas King, and Mr. and Mrs. John Parks (Ozona National Bank).   J.U.S.

ARTIST'S NOTES

This project began simply as an architectural treatment of some of the buildings which no longer exist on the forts around Texas. My thought was that these buildings were lost forever as a part of our visible history and that since it was within my ability to read and interpret old architectural plans, and "reconstruct" them in their original setting, this would be a way of recapturing history for people to visit and enjoy.

Many of the Texas frontier forts lay in complete ruin. For some, nothing was written down or preserved, and these are lost forever. But there were others that remained for a greater period of time, and at which permanent buildings were constructed from detailed architects' drawings which can be found today preserved in the National Archives in Washington, D.C. In addition, there were from time to time amateur artists among some of the soldiers; through research, some sketches have been found showing their interpretation of life on the forts. One such person was J. Howard, an enlisted man at Fort Griffin. He drew a series of primitive drawings of the officers' quarters, and from these the painting on this subject was created. The remainder of the research on the buildings was done mostly through several historical societies and through the Texas Parks and Wildlife Library, as well as the aforementioned National Archives (see the Acknowledgments).

As you view these paintings, you will find that some of the buildings are standing today. To my delight, some have been reconstructed since my project began. Every kind of building existing on a fort, except the stables and the powder magazine, has been re-created in at least one of the paintings. This was intended to give the viewer the idea that everything needed to "enjoy" a civilized existence was included on the fort—home, headquarters, commissary, hospital, mess hall, bakery, sutler's store (general store), library, school, and church. In order to include all these, I had to resort to painting a few buildings that are still standing.

But these walls were silent sentinels to Texas' historic past. While searching out old documents and historical data on the forts, I discovered and read several journals and diaries of soldiers and their wives. And when I traveled over Texas to visit the sites where the forts stood, the people I read about began to live again. In those remote areas, standing among the ruins, I could almost feel their presence and hear their voices on the wind. I could imagine the excitement at Fort Lancaster the day the camels arrived, and the gloom that settled over Fort Davis when the Flipper trial was in session at the chapel. There was the extremely harsh winter at Fort Richardson and the lonely feeling General Pershing must have felt living at Fort Bliss just after his wife and family perished in a terrible fire. I began to realize that just as important as re-creating the old buildings was reconstructing the life situations that these walls had witnessed, and my reason for the project became twofold, architectural and human.

Having been reared in the Christian faith and as the wife of a Presbyterian minister, I feel that all that we do has some purpose. I am not now certain what the real purpose of this book is, for it was not my intention originally to publish these paintings. A dear friend had the vision I did not have, and with her, and many others who, as a result of this book, have touched my life, it has been a walk of faith into a new and exciting dimension of life. What the ultimate purpose of this book is I may never know. But this I do know: these hardy people settled this land and endured its hardships and tragedies, and these walls surrounding them are a symbol to us of their strength and deep, abiding faith. Let us hope that history records our lives in the same way.   J.U.S.

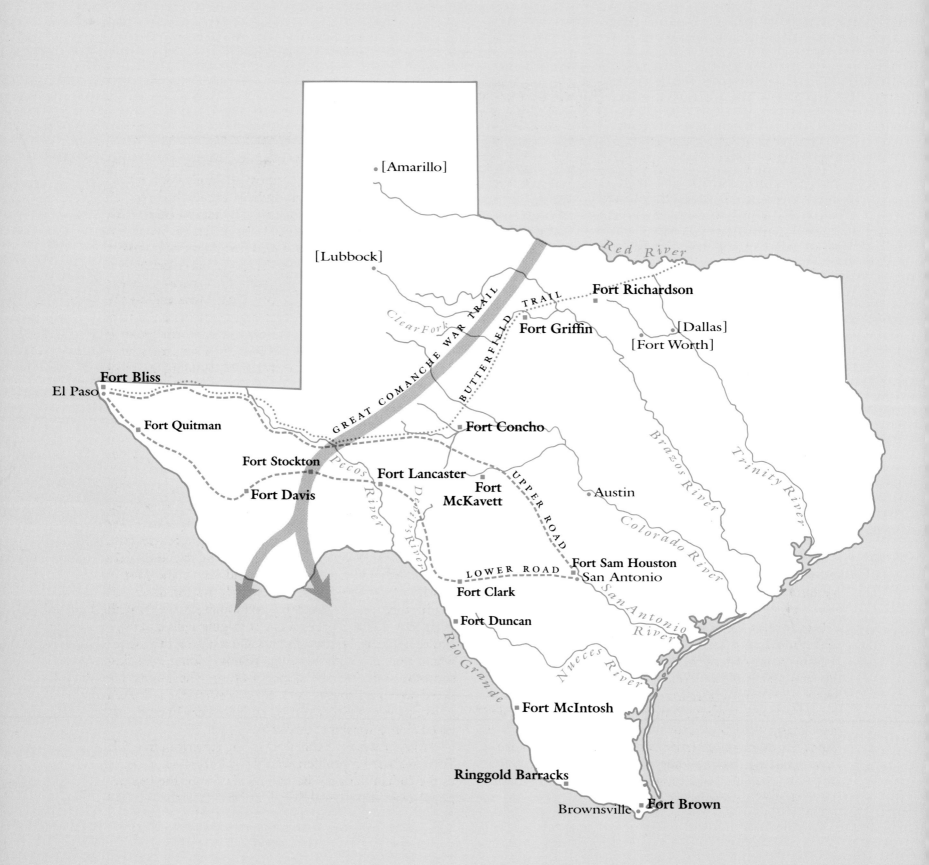

INTRODUCTION

All across Texas, crumbling walls mark the sites of military posts that once guarded the frontiers of settlement. If these walls could speak, they would tell an engrossing story—of people famous and anonymous, of events portentous and trivial, and above all of life—happy and tragic, gay and dull, busy and lethargic, always hard and deprived by the standards of the time but, even so, usually remembered with fond nostalgia by those who lived it. In fact, such walls may tell much more of history and life than commonly recognized, and beyond that they stand as symbols of a rich heritage. They are irreplaceable treasures that recall a significant and dramatic chapter in the opening of the American Southwest.

Not only in Texas, but wherever frontiers pushed westward, the military post played a vital role in the opening of new territory to settlement. Traders, prospectors, merchants, ranchers, farmers—all demanded the comforting sight of blue uniforms as they went about the business of conquering the wilderness. Up the Platte and the Arkansas as well as in Texas the little forts sprang to life. Along the Rio Grande in New Mexico, in California and the Pacific Northwest, and finally here and there amid the peaks and valleys of the Rockies, U.S. soldiers stamped their mark on the western landscape. The generals tried to shape their defensive systems with some regard for strategic requirements, but usually their fine theories yielded to democratic realities. The forts went where settlers and travelers felt threatened by Indians—and wanted a market for their produce and services. During the peak years of the westward movement—the two decades after the Civil War—more than a hundred such posts gave the illusion and sometimes the substance of protection to westering Americans and helped diminish and finally end the Indian menace. They also served as bases for more constructive achievements: for exploring new territory, for building roads and telegraphs, for strengthening local economies, and for enriching the society of nearby settlements.

Only a few of these forts resembled the familiar stockaded and bastioned outpost of Hollywood invention. With rare exceptions, Indians usually had enough sense not to attack an army installation, and only in the most exposed locations could any defensive works be seen. Rather, the typical western fort might be mistaken for an ordinary frontier town. The national colors floated from a tall, whitewashed flagstaff over a spacious parade ground fronted on one side by officers' row and on the other by enlisted men's barracks; but otherwise the various administrative offices, storehouses, and corrals were scattered about in random fashion. Most structures were hastily thrown together from whatever building materials the vicinity offered, usually stone, adobe, or rough lumber, and were distinguished chiefly by discomfort. Since forts tended to come and go with shifting frontiers and fluctuating Indian dangers, few were built to last, and their inhabitants despaired of ever escaping from wind, water, cold, dirt, and vermin.

Life at these forts, especially for families, held few attractions—except in nostalgic memories of friendships cemented and hardships shared. Beyond the rude living conditions, soldiers and their families suffered low pay, poor food, isolation, loneliness, boredom, strenuous field service, separation from friends and kin in the East, a paucity of civilized amenities, and always the danger of death or injury. But the Army community made do with what they had and grew adept at staging balls and hops and charades and festive dinners and amusing themselves where possible with hunting, fishing, riding, sporting contests, and other outdoor pastimes. The bugler ordered their daily routine, decreeing when to eat and when to work and when to sleep. A rigid hierarchy of rank governed all relationships, official and social.

More than any other part of the American frontier, Texas spawned a proliferation of these forts—a measure of the Indian danger, the restless vitality of the frontier population, and the state's political power in the national capital. Texas had no sooner joined the American union in 1845 than its spokesmen called insistently for federal help in fighting the Indians.

Indians were everywhere along the frontier and beyond. For generations, since the time of the first Spanish colonies, Kiowas and Comanches from north of the Red River had swept down on the Texas settlements and even carried their raids south of the Rio Grande deep into Mexico. From the mountains of southern New Mexico, Trans-Pecos Texas, and northern Mexico, Mescalero Apaches also struck at the frontier and joined with Kiowas and Comanches in preying on the travel routes that reached westward toward California. And finally, Lipans and Kickapoos stabbed across the new international border and scurried back to sanctuaries in the mountains of Coahuila.

For almost half a century after Texas became one of the United States, the Army and the Indian faced each other in the vast expanses of the state. Sometimes alone, sometimes sharing the task with Texas Rangers or improvised "minute man" units, the bluecoats patrolled the frontier and the travel routes, pursued Indian raiders, escorted mail carriers, stagecoaches, and freight and emigrant trains, and conducted exhausting campaigns into the home ranges of the enemy tribes. By the 1880s it was all over. The white soldiers had won. The crumbling walls and gaunt chimneys of their forts stood as reminders of the struggle and monuments to the victors as well as the vanquished.

The Mexican War had no sooner ended in 1848 than the federal government set about erecting a defense system for Texas. The task fell to General George M. Brooke, commander of the Eighth Military Department, which became the Department of Texas in 1853. At once he established a line of forts to guard the new international boundary along the Rio Grande—Forts Brown, Ringgold, McIntosh, and Duncan. These posts had the twin mission of policing the border and keeping Indian raiders out of the settlements. In these objectives they were aided by Fort Inge on the upper Frio River and, later, Forts Merrill and Ewell.

From the Rio Grande, Brooke then traced the frontier of settlement four hundred miles northward to the Red River. Slightly to the west, along the curving breaks of the Balcones Escarpment, he erected another chain of forts: Martin Scott on the Guadalupe River north of San Antonio, Croghan on the Colorado River above Austin, Graham and Gates on the Brazos River and a tributary, and Worth on the Trinity River.

Brooke's defense system, always lightly manned, failed utterly to turn aside Indian marauders. Indeed, in some ways it made matters worse. Settlers took confidence from the forts and pushed westward, into the path of the raiding parties. Also, these pioneers found at the forts a place to sell their beef and other produce, thus adding to the lure of the lands farther west. Within two years, the edge of settlement had left General Brooke's forts behind, and Texans demanded another defense line.

The architect of the new system was Brooke's successor, General Persifor F. Smith. Shielding the new frontier of settlement, the Smith line defined the western limit of reliable water flow in the rivers heading on the Staked Plains. By the end of 1852, Texans had an inner and outer cordon of forts with an intervening zone about 150 miles wide in which lay the edge of settlement. From north to south, the new bastions were Forts Belknap on the Brazos River, Phantom Hill on the Clear Fork of the Brazos, Chadbourne on a tributary of the upper Colorado, McKavett at the head of the San Saba, Terrett on the Llano River, and Clark, the southern anchor, on Las Moras Creek. Behind this line, between the San Saba and the Llano, Smith placed Fort Mason to give special protection to Fredericksburg and other German settlements that had been ravaged with unusual ferocity.

In addition to the inner and outer chains guarding the frontier of settlement and the Rio Grande border line, General Smith created still another line of forts. Two travel routes, the "Upper Road" and "Lower Road," linked San Antonio with El Paso across the desolate Trans-Pecos deserts. Feeding these roads was another from the northeast, soon to carry the coaches of the Butterfield Overland Mail. Converging into the main road across the Southwest to California, these trails bore mounting freight and emigrant traffic and offered an increasingly tempting target for Indian raiders. A new station at El Paso, Fort Bliss, provided protection to the western end of the roads. Farther east in 1854, General Smith established Fort Davis in the Limpia (Davis) Mountains. In 1855 he added Fort Lancaster near the crossing of the Pecos, and his successors filled in the chain with Camp Hudson (1857) at the crossing of Devil's River, Fort Quitman (1858) where the road touched the Rio Grande west of Fort Davis, and Fort Stockton (1859) at Comanche Springs, where the Lower Road to El Paso intersected the Great Comanche War Trail leading from the High Plains down into Mexico.

Such was the defense system from which the Army fought the Indians in the 1850s. There were campaigns and battles but mostly exhausting and profitless marches. Despite all the military activity, Indian raids did not diminish noticeably. At the outbreak of the Civil War, federal toops evacuated the forts. Weak Texas units occupied some of the posts and throughout the war made a show at contending with the Indians, but with even less result than the federals. When the bluecoats returned at war's end, the frontier had receded and continued to stagger under regular Indian forays. Once more the question of a defense system for Texas occupied military leaders.

Because of Reconstruction assignments, the federal troops did not get out on the frontier in strength until 1867. They began by reoccupying the old Smith system of forts. But officers were dissatisfied with many of them, some for sound strategic reasons, others for more mundane considerations of water, fuel, and building materials. Finally, in October 1867, a board of officers was named to examine the question and settle on locations. Based on their report, in February 1868 General Winfield S. Hancock, the Texas commander, issued orders for the new postwar system. Forts Belknap and Chadbourne would be abandoned and replaced by Forts Richardson at Jacksboro, Griffin on the Clear Fork of the Brazos, and Concho at the forks of the Concho River. From here the frontier line would extend to the Rio Grande by way of the reactivated prewar forts of McKavett, Terrett, Clark, and Duncan. McIntosh, Ringgold, and Brown would carry the line down the Rio Grande to the Gulf. Westward, Stockton, Davis, Quitman, and Bliss would, as before, guard the road to El Paso.

For the next fifteen years, General Hancock's network of forts supported military operations against the Indians. Texas was a hard land to fight in, and the Kiowas, Comanches, and Apaches were hard Indians to fight against. It was punishing duty, made the more disagreeable by the isolation and privations of the forts the soldiers called home. But the Red River War of 1874–1875, fought in part out of Texas forts, eliminated the Kiowa and Comanche menace; and the Victorio campaign of 1879–1880, based on Fort Davis and the other Trans-Pecos posts, ended Apache hostilities.

Throughout the era of the Indian Wars, and indeed for long after, the Army in Texas had also to contend with a troubled international frontier. Mexican politics, always volatile, spawned repeated revolutions that spilled across the boundary into Texas. American filibusters, based in the United States, pursued imperial adventures across the line. Bandits and smugglers from both nations kept the region in turmoil, while Indians from each country raided across the border, then retreated to safety while pursuers halted at the river. For a period in the 1870s, American military units played fast and loose with the doctrine of hot pursuit and, by conducting operations south of the boundary, brought Mexico and the United States to the verge of war. Again as late as 1917 U.S. troops crossed into Mexico as Pancho Villa and other revolutionaries or bandits wrought chaos and confusion along the border.

As they gradually prevailed over the Indians, the soldiers opened the way west for cowmen and settlers. Sometimes, in fact, the pioneers kept pace with the soldiers or even preceded them. They pastured their herds on the vast ranges of West Texas and transformed the wilderness with settled communities. The border garrisons found continuing service in policing the international frontier, but those that had struggled with Indians turned to other assignments. Most of their forts they simply abandoned. A few survived into the twentieth century, expanded to meet new needs, and finally succumbed. Of the thirty-three frontier forts that spotted Texas between 1845 and 1890, only Fort Sam Houston at San Antonio (1879) and Fort Bliss at El Paso have endured to the present as military installations. The rest have vanished altogether, or merged into the cities surrounding them, or found hands (and money) to preserve them for the inspiration and edification of modern generations, or simply fallen into ruins—ruins from which the old walls rise starkly, witnesses to adventure and tragedy and everyday life of the past but destined to carry their stories mutely with them as they, too, melt into the earth below.

SOURCES: Utley, *Frontiersmen in Blue* and *Frontier Regulars*.

14

FORT BROWN

Fort Brown had its origins in the opening maneuvers of the Mexican War. The United States' annexation of Texas precipitated a diplomatic crisis with Mexico and prompted President James K. Polk to order General Zachary Taylor to march his army of four thousand from Corpus Christi to the Rio Grande. Late in March 1846 Taylor established a base at Point Isabel, near the river's mouth, and moved his army upstream thirty miles to confront the large Mexican force at Matamoros. On the north bank of the river, opposite the town, Taylor's men erected a flagpole, hoisted the colors in token of possession, and began throwing up a defensive work—the classic fortification of European design, constructed of earthen mounds and shaped like a star.

Hostilities broke out three weeks later. Taylor, fearing for his base at the mouth of the Rio Grande, left Major Jacob Brown and about five hundred men to hold the fort and led his force hastily downstream. The Mexicans promptly laid siege to the fort and opened fire with artillery. For six days they blasted away at the American defenders while Taylor rushed back to their aid. On May 8 and 9 he met and routed the main Mexican army at the Battles of Palo Alto and Resaca de la Palma, then marched back to the battered fort. Here he learned that, midway through the bombardment, an artillery round had shattered Major Brown's leg. It had been amputated, but after lingering for three days he had died. To honor his memory, Taylor named the defensive work Fort Brown, and the city that soon sprang up nearby took the name Brownsville.

After the Mexican War, late in 1848, U.S. troops returned to the site, and next to the earthen fort they began work on a permanent post. It was an appealing location. A perfectly level alluvial bottom, covered thickly with chaparral, it boasted handsome trees and irrigating aqueducts, now falling into ruin, that testified to previous development by some Spanish grandee. A large lake or lagoon, remnant of an abandoned river bed, surrounded a twenty-five-acre island where the soldiers raised a flagstaff and laid out a cemetery for Mexican War dead. An officer's wife passing through in 1850 looked upon Fort Brown and concluded: "Its well kept fences, and regularly placed barracks and buildings, with the vine-covered cottages that form the officers' quarters, add in no small degree to the beauty and importance of Brownsville; while the daily guard-mountings, parades, and drills, and the accompanying military music, add greatly to the feelings of safety and importance of its citizens."

With its sister posts on the Rio Grande line, Fort Brown guarded the international frontier and sought to impose a semblance of security on a land troubled by American filibusters against Mexico, Mexican revolutionaries, bandits and desperadoes of both nations, and even an occasional Indian raiding party that slipped through the frontier defenses to the west.

The most serious disturbances occurred in 1859, at a time when this frontier lay dangerously exposed. Indian troubles far to the north had emptied the southern forts, including Fort Brown. Juan Nepomuceno Cortina, a fearless combination of patriot and brigand whose red beard and fair complexion gave him an un-Mexican aspect, chose this moment to spearhead a revolt against the Americans of the lower Rio Grande. He sought to strike down the racial and economic oppression from which his people suffered and also, in the process, to visit a bit of plunder of his own on the oppressors. Violence and pillage rocked the lower valley for two months. At one point Cortina even made his headquarters at Fort Brown and hoisted the Mexican ensign on the fort's flagpole. Finally, in December 1859, Texas Rangers and U.S. regulars rushed to the scene and broke up the insurgent "army" of several hundred men. Cortina himself eluded capture, but when a new U.S. commander took over in Texas he let the Mexican authorities know that they must control their unruly countrymen or he, Colonel Robert E. Lee, would come across the border and do it for them. Juan Cortina hardly vanished from history, but the Cortina "War" of 1859 had ended.

Though remote from eastern battlefields, Fort Brown figured importantly in the Civil War. U.S. troops withdrew in the spring of 1861, and Confederates took their place. Because of the strategic significance of the Mexican frontier, they held Fort Brown and the other river posts in considerable strength. The Union blockade of the South's ports made Brownsville and Matamoros a great funnel through which poured southern cotton in exchange for European armaments and supplies of war. Sleek blockade runners darted through the patrolling Yankee squadrons and made their way up the river to Matamoros, while freight trains crawled southward to other Mexican ports and northward to the gray armies struggling in the East.

To sever this lifeline, a large federal force landed at Point Isabel in November 1863. Greatly outnumbered, General H. P. Bee put the torch to Fort Brown and withdrew. The fire not only destroyed the buildings but blazed out of control and obliterated part of Brownsville. Federals occupied the wrecked fort until the summer of 1864, when they withdrew to Point Isabel.

Meantime, across the river, French invaders and their puppet emperor, Maximilian, challenged the tottering government of Benito Juárez. A French army advanced on Matamoros. The Juarista commander, none other than General Juan Nepomuceno Cortina, turned them back. Then he brushed aside a Confederate force that tried to intervene, raised the U.S. flag over Fort Brown, and sent word to the senior U.S. officer at Point Isabel to come repossess his fort. Commanding only a weak force, that worthy had to decline.

With the lower river the setting for a volatile mixture of Yankees, Confederates, Mexicans in bewildering factional variety, French imperialists, and plain oppor-

tunists, it is no wonder that the Civil War history of Fort Brown and its environs is confusing and mystifying. As a final curiosity, the last battle of the Civil War was fought only a few miles from Fort Brown. It was a Confederate victory, but it had no effect on the course of the war, for the date was May 13, 1865; unknown to the combatants, Lee had surrendered at Appomattox more than a month earlier.

United States soldiers came back after the war. The first made up General Philip H. Sheridan's "Army of Observation," fifty thousand Union veterans sent to the Rio Grande to make plain to the French what the United States thought about their pretensions in Mexico. After Maximilian's collapse, regulars settled into their military routine at Fort Brown. Once more temporary huts went up while more enduring structures were under construction. But in 1867 a hurricane wiped out both old and new, and the project had to be started all over again.

The buildings that now sprouted in military order around the lagoon and along the river's edge were solid, spacious, and comfortable. Some were frame, others brick. Porches afforded retreat from the tropical sun and, creating deep shadows, enhanced the visual appeal. It was a big post, with dozens of buildings. Infantry, artillery, and cavalry each had its own compound. The lagoon served utilitarian as well as esthetic purposes: it provided a convenient bathtub for the garrison.

As the decades passed, Fort Brown gradually acquired a reputation as one of the most desirable assignments the army could offer. Southeast trade winds abated the summer's fierce heat, and winters were mild and sunny. Hunting and fishing held rich appeal for sportsmen. Brownsville afforded city amenities and a congenial civilian society. Even the fevers that kept the hospital busy diminished as surgeons learned how to cope and commanders instituted sanitary measures. The Mexican border troubles just before World War I brought new but transitory life and importance to the fort. A hurricane in

BACHELOR OFFICERS' QUARTERS, FORT BROWN

With walls three feet thick to offer relief from summer heat, the combination Tudor and Victorian style
buildings housed eight officers comfortably. The water cistern and kitchen are attached to the rear of the
building, and stables were conveniently located near the quarters.

1933 wiped out most of the frame buildings; the brick ones stood, and, as in the past, reconstruction began at once.

Thus Fort Brown lived out its long life quietly and routinely. Not until 1944 did the last garrison march away, leaving the buildings to a variety of civilian uses. They still stand, reminders of a long and distinguished history. And downstream a short distance the careful observer may still pick out the mounded outlines of Major Brown's earthen fort, where that history began.

SOURCES: Billings, *Report on Barracks* and *Report on Hygiene*; Crimmins, "First Line"; Crimmins, ed., "Freeman's Report" and "Mansfield's Report"; Frazer, *Forts of the West*; Prucha, *Guide*; Viele, *Following the Drum*; Webb, *Texas Rangers*.

RINGGOLD BARRACKS

Upriver 125 miles from Fort Brown stood the second of the Rio Grande border posts, Ringgold Barracks, named in honor of a dashing artillery captain in Zachary Taylor's army who had been killed in the Battle of Palo Alto. This post was established in October 1848 at Davis Landing, the head of navigation on the Rio Grande, and lay opposite the Mexican town of Camargo. Davis Landing soon became the community of Rio Grande City.

The locale of Ringgold Barracks held little of appeal. The sterile, sandy soil supported mesquite and prickly pear cactus but little else save rattlers, centipedes, scorpions, and tarantulas. Winters featured pleasant temperatures, and sea breezes blowing inland from the Gulf at night made the summers bearable, but the still, torrid daytime stifled human activity. Nor was the human population to be especially admired. "Holding out such meager inducements," noted a later observer, "this vicinity has drawn principally from our country the non-producer, the adventurer, who chafes under the restraints of civilization, and others of that ilk."

To Ringgold Barracks in 1850, shortly after its founding, came a young infantry lieutenant with the improbable name of Egbert Ludovickus Viele, and with him to this, her first military station, came his young wife, Theresa. Product of a cultured eastern upbringing, she soaked up literature and the arts, took comfort in high-church connections, looked with assured condescension on Mexicans and blacks, and regarded Indians with terror and loathing. For all her refinement, however, she could also take the privations and hardships in her stride and approach her life far from upholstered drawing rooms in a spirit of adventure and learning.

As Lieutenant and Mrs. Viele debarked from the steamer that brought them up the Rio Grande from Brownsville, they looked for the first time on their new home. It "rose before us on a high sandy bluff," she later wrote, "its rows of long, low, white-washed modern buildings placed at regular intervals around a level drill ground, in the center of which rose the flag-staff, with its colors hanging droopingly, unstirred by the sultry air. These buildings were the government store-houses, soldiers' barracks, and officers' quarters; they all reminded me of the house of the foolish man, 'who built his foundation upon the sand,' all being in similar plight. There were no signs of vegetation around; not even a blade of grass was to be seen. The sentinels monotonously walking guard gave unmistakable token of a military post."

To Theresa Viele posterity is indebted for glimpses of life on the lower Rio Grande at mid-century. The hot winds, the swirling dust, the venomous red ants that got into the food and tasted like caraway seeds, the warm and muddy river water that hardly quenched thirst, the runny butter that could never be made firm, the commissary's moldy flour and rancid pork that constituted the daily diet when the river fell and the supply steamer could not reach the post, and the scrawny horse that was all ribs, resisted the fattening process, and succumbed at last, almost unbelievably, to a death induced by swallowing a wine glass—all came under her careful scrutiny, and all came to life under her graphic pen.

To Theresa Viele fell the good fortune to meet one of the frontier Army's legendary characters, General William S. Harney. Huge-framed, full-bearded, hot-tempered, scarred veteran of the Seminole Wars and the Mexican War, he was the subject of many an anecdote throughout the Army. As Texas commander, he came to Ringgold on the inspection tour. "Even in these wild regions," wrote Theresa Viele, "Harney's dragoons rode into camp in full equipment, on prancing horses, with their carbines and sabers glistening in the early morning sunlight."

Characteristically, Harney furnished grist for yet another anecdote. Mexican officers came across from Camargo to pay their respects. While they were visiting with Harney in the commanding officer's quarters, orderlies attended their splendidly equipped mounts outside. But briefly the orderlies succumbed to the hospitality of the enlisted mess, and when they returned someone had made off with the silver-mounted pistols holstered on the Mexican horses. Chagrined, the American officers made embarrassed apologies. Next day the thief was found to be one of Harney's own dragoons. Theresa Viele watched as the general, "a man of tremendous physique and strong impetuous passions," confronted the soldier on the front porch of the commanding officer's quarters. "He seized the culprit by the nape of the neck, like a kitten, and administered a good shaking and moral lecture combined." One suspects that Harney's "moral lecture" could not have withstood a clergyman's scrutiny.

Ringgold Barracks watched over a troubled border and did its part in trying to cope with the Indian menace, chiefly Comanches from the north preying on the exposed settlements of Texas and Mexico. It also figured in the filibustering of José María Carvajal and the violence inspired by Juan Nepomuceno Cortina. The Ringgold garrison watched nervously as Carvajal, with a mixed following of Mexican and American adventurers, twice laid siege to Camargo, across the river. Thus strategically located, Ringgold Barracks was looked upon by military authorities as an important post.

Although not strong in numbers, the troops assigned to Ringgold Barracks during the 1850s were among the best in the Army. They mightily impressed an inspecting officer in 1853: "The erect carriage of the infantry, their stead-

iness in the ranks, their trim fitting clothing and the scrupulous neatness of their arms and accoutrements, all gave evidence of a high state of discipline and instruction. The cavalry also was in fine order, their horses well groomed and equipments neatly cleaned. . . . Indeed in soldierly bearing and punctual attention to all the duties prescribed by the Regulations, this garrison stands preeminent."

Abandoned at the outbreak of the Civil War, Ringgold Barracks was regarrisoned when the bluecoats returned in 1865. Construction of a new fort began in the early 1870s, but the project was never completed, and the old buildings continued to serve along with the new. In 1878 the Army renamed the post Fort Ringgold. Inactivated in 1906, it took on new life during the Mexican border troubles of 1913–1917. Finally, in 1944, Ringgold was abandoned for good and its buildings, like those of Fort Brown, devoted to nonmilitary uses. Most may still be seen in Rio Grande City.

Ringgold Barracks, and all such remote and forbidding frontier forts, left those who served there with bittersweet memories. Theresa Viele ended her tour at Ringgold Barrracks "with as much pain as pleasure," as she wrote. "I left behind me warm hearts, and brought with me sweet memories, and new and enlarged views of life as it really is."

SOURCES: Billings, *Report on Barracks* and *Report on Hygiene*; Crimmins, "First Line"; Crimmins, ed., "Freeman's Report" and "Mansfield's Report"; Frazer, *Forts of the West*; Prucha, *Guide*; Viele, *Following the Drum*; Webb, *Texas Rangers*.

(opposite page)

HOSPITAL AND ENLISTED MEN'S BARRACKS, RINGGOLD BARRACKS
Although the floor plans for the barracks and hospital are the same as for many of the forts built during this era, the Army chose the Moorish architectural style and adobe masonry common to the area.

FORT RINGOLD

FORT MCINTOSH

Another of the string of border forts guarding the Rio Grande frontier with Mexico, Fort McIntosh nestled in a crook of the river 118 miles upstream from Ringgold Barracks. Established in 1849, it occupied a plain some fifty feet above the river and composed mainly of loose sand, mesquite, and prickly pear. Laredo, a century-old city of a thousand people, lay on the opposite side of the river, and a tiny community of Americans, later to take the name of New Laredo, took shape on the north bank less than a mile upstream. Along with its sister posts, Fort McIntosh watched over the international boundary and contended against raiding Indians.

Fort McIntosh enjoyed a long life—almost a hundred years—but gained the maturity of comfortable, durable buildings only when long past its prime. It began as an earthen star fort on the Fort Brown pattern, designed and constructed by one of the Army's ablest engineers, Major Richard Delafield. From its embrasures, cannon commanded the river and the Mexican town on the other side. But the artillery never fired in hostility, and the fortification never justified its formidable aspect. Meantime, the garrison had to make do in tents, throw up brush arbors on poles to protect themselves and their horses from the fierce sun, and cook and eat their meals in the open. Orders from a department commander uncertain of the fort's future prohibited expenditures for permanent buildings. Even the poles for the arbors, scarce and costly in this timberless land, had to be purchased out of the company funds, which consisted of money belonging properly to the soldiers themselves. When the poles rotted and the shelters collapsed, these coffers turned out to be empty. "The thermometer stood at 99 degrees," reported a visiting inspector in 1856, and "the suffering of both man and horse was great."

Disgusted with such conditions, two officers set about to erect a set of officers' quarters with their own money. The same inspector, however, frowned on this solution as damaging to morale and suggested that no further buildings be built for officers until the enlisted men could be taken out of their tents. "I do not consider this small field fort of any material strength or importance," he observed. "The same labour would have put the men in comfortable quarters."

Abundant sandstone for comfortable quarters existed in the low hills that rose from the plain scarcely two miles to the north. Not until after the Confederate interlude, however, did authority arrive to quarry building blocks and construct a lasting installation. In 1868 work commenced on a new post, about half a mile downstream and some four hundred yards from the river bank. A substantial stone hospital, guardhouse, bakery, and storehouse were completed, but the money ran out and work ceased before the "comfortable quarters" were even begun. The officers then moved into the hospital and part of the troops into the storehouse, while the balance continued, as for two decades past, to live in tents. Not until years later did the flow of funds resume and Fort McIntosh reach its ultimate dimensions.

The quality of life at Fort McIntosh resembled that at its sister posts downstream. The climate was much the same, on the whole benign despite summer heat. Locally grown produce and the attractions of the frontier metropolis across the river lent variety and amenity to life. As always, the water supply aroused complaint. In the spring and fall of each year, observed a post surgeon, "the river water becomes so muddy as to form nearly a paste, and only after continued filtration is it comparatively fit for domestic use." Another surgeon, however, reported that a little alum stirred into a barrel of water would "render it in a few minutes as clear as spring water." And if alum could not be had, "A piece of the prickly pear has the same effect."

GUARDHOUSE, FORT MCINTOSH

This building still stands but has been altered. According to the original architectural drawings, this is the way
it was originally constructed: on the right (small windows) are the cells and on the left the receiving rooms.

ENLISTED MEN'S BARRACKS, FORT MCINTOSH

Built of materials available in the area, these barracks are typical two-story buildings with wide porches on both sides. The fort chapel
is in the background. Also note the palm trees (which are found on all forts along the Rio Grande) planted by the Army and still there today.

The country around Fort McIntosh afforded superb hunting. "It was a great pasture for thousands of wild horses, and wild cattle, deer, antelope, and every game bird we know of, and every sort of predatory beast," recalled Lieutenant Dabney H. Maury, a Virginian of distinguished lineage soon to become a Confederate general. He gloried in many hunting adventures with all kinds of game, but the most challenging quarry he found to be wild cattle.

Once, in charge of grazing his squadron's horses on fresh grass downstream from Fort McIntosh, Maury, a Mexican guide, and two soldiers got on the trail of a huge white bull, a veritable "monarch of the herds." Pursuing for two hours, the party finally cornered the beast in a clump of bushes and wounded him. He bolted into the open and, trailing blood, loped off across the desert. Half an hour later he took two more balls, and Maury dismounted and closed in for the kill. Suddenly one of the men shouted, "Look out, Lieutenant! He is charging you!"

Out of a thicket crashed the bull as the officer turned and dashed for his horse. Hearing hooves pounding on his very heels, Maury threw himself into a great clump of cactus, emerging on the other side full of painful thorns. Pulling himself up, he heard another shouted warning, and once more he jumped into a cactus bed. Now he fairly bristled with thorns. "They are the size of a large darning needle, with barbed points, and when one is pulled out it leaves the barb in to mark the place." Now Maury rose more cautiously. His rifle was empty, his companions gone, his horse gone, and, mercifully, the bull gone; "but alas! the cactus spikes remained!"

Fort McIntosh played its part in shielding the settlements from Indian raiders, chiefly in the 1850s. The threat came from Comanches on their long sweeping raids from distant northern ranges and from tribes living in Mexico, prominent among them the Lipan Apaches. Mounted infantry scouted the country for sign of Comanche war parties. One such expedition, in April 1850, closed with the usually elusive quarry. Lieutenant Walter Hudson commanded, and in the sharp, furious fight, as his men later explained, he was on the point of shooting an Indian when he noted that he had a woman in his sights. He lowered his pistol, and the woman spurred her horse and impaled him on a spear. As he died, a sergeant took command and the enraged soldiers made short work of the adversaries, including the woman.

Later in the 1850s horse soldiers came to the Rio Grande forts to replace the infantrymen and their mules. Lieutenant Maury's outfit, the Regiment of Mounted Riflemen, scouted and campaigned strenuously to head off the forays of Lipans into Texas. Finally, McIntosh's commander, Captain Daniel Ruggles, persuaded Mexican authorities to police their own Indians. In the face of aggressive Mexican offensives, some fled to the United States side of the Rio Grande, but a mounted command under Lieutenant Gordon Granger, in a three-week scout of seven hundred miles, overtook and severely chastised them.

By comparison with the 1850s, the years after the Civil War were placid, with little hard service or danger. At last the fine new buildings of stone gave the troops release from their stifling tents. Except for the excitement of the border troubles just before World War I, Fort McIntosh lingered peacefully until after World War II. Not until 1946, two years after relinquishing the sister posts of Brown and Ringgold, did the Army march out of Fort McIntosh for the last time. Its buildings, on the west side of modern Laredo, serve civilian purposes but also capture the flavor of earlier times.

SOURCES: Billings, *Report on Barracks* and *Report on Hygiene*; Crimmins, "First Line"; Crimmins, ed., "Freeman's Report" and "Mansfield's Report"; Frazer, *Forts of the West*; Maury, *Recollections*; Prucha, *Guide*; Viele, *Following the Drum*; Webb, *Texas Rangers*.

SUTLER'S STORE, FORT MCINTOSH
The "supermarket" of its time, the store was usually owned by a civilian. However, according to archival records, this one was bought by the Army and remodeled.

FORT MCKAVETT

When General Persifor Smith reorganized the Texas frontier defenses in 1851, he designed Fort McKavett as a key link in the "outer chain" and planted it, lonely but defiant, a hundred miles in advance of the line of settlement and squarely in the path of Kiowa and Comanche war parties riding down from the north. Before and after the Civil War, Fort McKavett held its sector of the line without ostentation or excitement. The Indians usually avoided or eluded the routine scouts and patrols that occupied its garrison, while the accidents of war awarded to its sister posts the eye-catching field service and combat. At the same time, it evolved into one of the most solid, comfortable, and beautifully situated stations in Texas.

Men and women who lived there remembered McKavett as a pleasant interlude marred only by the extreme isolation. All supplies had to be hauled from San Antonio, distant 180 miles. The nearest civilians in the 1850s made their homes in the German town of Fredericksburg, 100 miles to the east.

Elements of the Eighth U.S. Infantry under Major Pitcairn Morrison selected the site for Fort McKavett in March 1852 atop a stony plateau overlooking the head streams of the San Saba River. Hills and valleys rolled off in all directions, their slopes colored by rich grasses, mesquite, and stunted live oaks. Stately walnut, pecan, and willow trees traced the course of the river curving around the bluff north and west of the post.

The neighborhood yielded abundant limestone, which the infantrymen quarried and cut into irregular building blocks from which to erect barracks, officers' quarters, hospital, guardhouse, and storehouses. From the beginning, therefore, Fort McKavett took on an aura of stability and permanence uncharacteristic of the dilapidated forts usually thrown together in the Indian country. Around a level parade ground, it rose compact and fortresslike, ready for defense if necessary but as comfortable as shelters could be on a distant frontier.

With other forts on the outer line, Fort McKavett marked the western limit of reliable water. But reliable the water was. In addition to the river's constant flow, a spring bubbled up at the base of a cliff just west of the post to provide clear, cold water for cooking and washing. The surgeon considered it healthful even though tasting strongly of lime. The spring and the river created two swampy lakes, or lagoons, that the men used for bathing in warm weather and that also fed water into a network of irrigating ditches for the post vegetable garden. Thirty acres in size, it furnished the garrison a steady supply of melons, cantaloupe, squash, pumpkin, sweet potatoes, and other produce and seemed to confirm a surgeon's judgment in later years that "The valley of the San Saba is a garden, waiting to be planted."

Construction was well advanced by August 1853, when Lieutenant Colonel W. G. Freeman visited Fort McKavett for the Inspector General's Department. For the most part, he liked what he saw and judged the staff departments well managed. In the five infantry companies, however, "I found military instruction invariably subordinated, perhaps necessarily, to the labours of the axe, saw and hammer." Moreover, armed with various makes of rifles and muskets and clothed in a mix of the old and new patterns of uniform, the troops made a sloppy appearance. Adding to the disorder, some of the footmen had horses while the rest paraded on foot. Freeman hoped the horses might be done away with altogether, "for it is now everywhere conceded that the experiment of mounting infantry has not been successful." Curiously, only three years later another inspecting officer concluded that two companies of infantry would be sufficient for McKavett so long as enough mules were kept on hand to mount the soldiers for field service.

Along with other Texas posts, Fort McKavett was held by Confederates during the Civil War years. Federal troops did not return until the spring of 1868, and by then the buildings had fallen into ruin. Only the commanding

COMMANDING OFFICER'S QUARTERS, FORT MCKAVETT

This was a grand home for its location and time. The view is toward the rear of the house, showing the kitchen and attached stable on the left and the commander's study on the right. The smaller of the two parade grounds can be seen in the background.

SCHOOL, FORT MCKAVETT

It is autumn, and school is in session. Classes were taught by officers or their wives, whoever was best qualified at the time.

officer's house was habitable, and that only because the settler who claimed the land made his residence there and kept up the premises.

Fort McKavett owed its renaissance to a man destined to become one of the frontier Army's most notable celebrities. Ranald S. Mackenzie came to Fort McKavett in March 1869 as colonel of the Forty-first U.S. Infantry. Not yet thirty years old, he had served with distinction in the Civil War and risen to brigadier general of volunteers. Here at Fort McKavett this brilliant field soldier and strict disciplinarian, quick of temper and nervous of disposition, began an association with Texas that was to last through the 1870s and achieve surpassing influence in opening the state's vast western lands to white settlement.

Mackenzie's regiment, which army reorganization almost immediately transformed into the Twenty-fourth, was one of four new regular army units composed of black soldiers and white officers. At Fort McKavett, Mackenzie began laying the groundwork for the regiment's eventual development into one of the Army's proudest outfits. He also set about rebuilding the fort.

Over the next five years, under the superintendence of Mackenzie and successive commanders, Fort McKavett's stone edifices were reconstructed, enlarged, and embellished. New ones went up, too. The commanding officer's quarters, with two stories, shaded verandas, and attractive lattices, dominated officers' row and prompted an observer to brand them "elegant in every respect." The post garden once more yielded fine fresh vegetables. By 1875, Fort McKavett had become one of the handsomest and most comfortable installations in all Texas. "There is no more healthy post on the Texas frontier than Fort McKavett," declared the surgeon, who doubtless did not include in his assessment the scraggly assemblage of pleasure pots in the valley below, called Scabtown, from which emanated much of his hospital's patronage.

About the only complaint that could be made was the expense of transporting the amenities of civilization from Austin and San Antonio. And of course there was that perennial lament of officers' wives throughout the western army that suitable servants were not to be had. As usual the perceptive surgeon gave voice to it: "Female servants are most difficult to get from either Austin, San Antonio, or Fredericksburgh, as it is deemed disreputable for them to come to a garrison filled with soldiers." Those who did come quickly found their way out of the kitchen and, hand in hand with some lonely soldier, to the chaplain's altar.

In December 1870 Mackenzie left Fort McKavett and the Twenty-fourth Infantry to take command of the Fourth Cavalry, a choice assignment seemingly decreed by an admiring President U. S. Grant himself. Under Mackenzie, the Fourth wrote a record of adventure and achievement from the Staked Plains to the Rio Grande and even, at the risk of foreign war, into Mexico. With his new regiment, therefore, he had occasion now and then to pass through Fort McKavett and admire the handiwork he had begun.

One such visit occurred on a wet day early in 1873, when the Fourth paused there on a long march from the north to new stations on the Mexican border. The post commander, Lieutenant Colonel A. McD. McCook, persuaded the always restless Mackenzie to let his regiment rest for a couple of days. The highlight of the stay was "an old fashioned frontier hop" staged by McCook and his Tenth Infantry officers for the visiting cavalrymen. Despite limitations of wardrobe, all turned out in dazzling regalia. "It was a revelation how the ladies managed to secure so much finery in such a short time," observed a cavalry officer, "but we always suspected that most of it was borrowed from their generous hostesses of the Fort McKavett garrison." Colonel McCook turned out to be the star of the evening, as he danced "La Paloma" under an enormous white sombrero sporting his name on the brim in silver and gold bullion, a gift of the citizens of Matamoros.

It is perhaps fitting that such images are more characteristic of Fort McKavett than the clash of arms or grueling pursuits of Indians. Together with an attractive setting, healthful climate, comfortable dwellings, and amenities of diet unknown at most other forts, the relative freedom from danger and hardship seems somehow appropriate. A tour at McKavett thus offered respite from the demands and sacrifices of life at more typical frontier forts. Throughout the 1870s the solid stone fort on the San Saba watched over its sector of the frontier. Finally, on June 30, 1883, the flag came down for the last time.

Today Fort McKavett State Historic Park embraces impressive stone remains, consisting of crumbling walls overgrown with weeds and original structures adapted to modern uses. They are scattered throughout the town of Fort McKavett.

SOURCES: Billings, *Report on Barracks* and *Report on Hygiene;* Carter, *On the Border;* Crimmins, ed., "Freeman's Report" and "Mansfield's Report"; Frazer, *Forts of the West;* Holden, "Frontier Defense"; Leckie, *Buffalo Soldiers;* Prucha, *Guide.*

ENLISTED MEN'S BARRACKS, FORT LANCASTER
The "Camel Corps" has arrived and all is chaos. Note the laundresses' huts at the left rear. These women were
usually wives of enlisted men. Headquarters and sutler's store are at right rear beside the San Antonio–El Paso stage road.

FORT LANCASTER

One of the guardians of the San Antonio–El Paso Road, Fort Lancaster held the forbidding stretch of the route from the head of Devil's River to the flat desert plain beyond the Pecos. This "Lower Road" to the west, shorter and more popular than the "Upper Road," bore mounting traffic during the 1850s and suffered increasingly destructive and lethal depredations from Comanche and Apache raiders. Fort Lancaster, established in August 1855 where the road crossed the Pecos, strove valiantly to turn aside these forays.

For lonely isolation, desolate setting, and constant threat of death or mutilation, few Texas forts could match Fort Lancaster. It lay on the east bank of Live Oak Creek half a mile from its confluence with the Pecos. Yucca, creosote bush, and a thin burro grass rooted in rocky, sandy soil covered the level valley floor. Along its western edge, an intermittent thread of green—cottonwoods and live oak—traced the course of the Pecos. To the east a rampart of barren hills and rugged canyons, capped with great buff boulders and spotted with lechuguilla and struggling scrub cedars, shouldered the valley and lifted the wagon road in twisting loops to the plain above. Southward the road pointed 175 tortuous miles to Fort Clark and on to San Antonio, and westward it stretched across 158 desert miles to Fort Davis. Hot wind and sun blasted the site in summer, and northers swept down on it in winter. Indians haunted the vicinity; whites ventured beyond the parade ground at their peril.

Two companies of the First U.S. Infantry, first under Captain Stephen D. Carpenter, later under Captain Robert S. Granger, built and manned Fort Lancaster. It was a rudely constructed post, affording primitive living conditions at best. The walls of some of the buildings were made of roughly hewn limestone quarried nearby and roofed first with canvas, later with grass thatching. Four sets of officers' quarters, stone structures with separate adobe kitchens, looked eastward across the dusty parade ground with its flagpole bravely flaunting the national colors. Facing the parade on the east stood the adjutant's office, backed by storehouses and other utility structures, and flanked on each side by barracks and kitchens for the enlisted men.

These barracks were a mixture of stone buildings with canvas or thatched roofs and the so-called "Turnley cottages." An early attempt at prefabricated construction, the Turnley cottage consisted of a precut portable frame, pine planks for siding, and tent canvas to fasten over the top for a roof. "They would have been rather satisfactory," judged an early observer, "if the winds had not been severe. This necessitated bracing and propping them." Also, the long, rough wagon trip from San Antonio damaged some of the kits.

Colonel J. K. F. Mansfield inspected Fort Lancaster in 1856, a year after its establishment. He found the two infantry companies reasonably well disciplined and drilled, considering the scarcity of officers and the high proportion of recruits. The guardhouse, an insubstantial pole jacal, held seventy-six prisoners, fifteen of them confined for drunkenness. The liquor came from travelers, not the post sutler, who could sell "ardent spirits" only under permit from the commanding officer. "I presume the great error," concluded the colonel, "is in enlisting confirmed drunkards who desire nothing better than to get drunk & lay in the guard house."

Colonel Mansfield gave special thought to the Indian menace. On the way up from Fort Clark his escort had rescued a demoralized freight train that had been attacked by Indians the day before. "They keep out of sight & commit depredations & murders at times when least expected," he wrote. Fort Lancaster was important and well located to protect the Pecos segment of the road. Also, two companies were an adequate force here. But they should have all their officers. They should have mules, "so as to be able to trail Indians after they had committed depredations and follow them up." And they should be equipped with the new rifled muskets recently adopted by the army, "for Indians when running must be reached at a long range, up the mountains &c., or not at all."

Fort Lancaster took on even greater significance in 1857, with the inauguration of the San Antonio–San Diego Mail—the famed "Jackass Mail." James H. Giddings had run monthly coaches to El Paso and Santa Fe since 1853. Now, as agent for the eastern division of the Jackass Mail, Giddings in addition operated twice-monthly service to El Paso with Concord coaches.

Fort Lancaster's infantrymen spent much of their time in the arduous, unspectacular duty of escorting mail coaches and freight trains, pursuing but rarely catching raiders who had attacked travelers or a mail station, and combing their sector with scouts that were usually unrewarding. Occasionally there was action, but it involved small numbers on both sides.

One exciting episode occurred in the summer of 1857, a time of especially intense hostility. On July 24 about eighty Apache warriors jumped a fourteen-man detachment with two wagons twenty-five miles west of Fort Lancaster. Abandoning the wagons and the body of a slain sergeant, the infantrymen dashed back to the fort while the Indians paused to plunder the wagons and scalp the sergeant. At Fort Lancaster Captain Granger organized a pursuing force of eighty men from his own command and a party of Fort Davis troops that happened to be at the post. Lieutenant Edward Hartz, in command, loaded the men in wagons, drew the canvas covers, and set forth on the road under the guise of a provision train. The Indians took the bait and about forty-five miles to the west swept down on the train. The soldiers piled out of the wagons, opened fire, and brought down three of the attackers before they discovered what had happened and pulled back out of range.

Next the Apaches fired the prairie grass, hoping to destroy the train and create a smoke screen under which to mount another attack. But Hartz moved the wagons into a grassless depression and had his men lie on their faces. When the wall of flame had moved on, the troops again advanced, firing with such effect that the Indians gave up the fight and withdrew. Meeting the eastbound mail, Hartz' men turned and escorted it back to Fort Lancaster.

The road through Fort Lancaster bore the hoof-prints of horses, mules, oxen, and even cattle and sheep, but strangest of all were the cloven marks of the camel. Secretary of War Jefferson Davis sponsored experiments with camels as beasts of burden for military use in the desert Southwest. An officer with one such expedition that came through Fort Lancaster in 1857 marveled at the endurance and strength of these animals. On such a road, he said, in such heat, and without water, mules would go wild and break down entirely. The camels pulled through serenely and effortlessly. In both 1859 and 1860, in the desert mountains southwest of Lancaster, comparative tests were conducted using both camels and mules, with the camels invariably demonstrating clear superiority. But the Civil War ended the experiments and scattered the camels, and the legendary army mule soon reasserted its supremacy in the affections of soldier and civilian alike.

Despite its strategic location, Fort Lancaster turned out to be short lived. At the outbreak of the Civil War, the federal garrison marched away. A skeleton Confederate unit occupied the fort but evacuated after only a year, leaving the buildings deserted and deteriorating. Unlike other Texas forts, Lancaster was not re-established after the war, although it served on occasion, for brief periods, as a subpost to other forts in the campaigns of the post-war decade. No use is recorded after 1874, and the buildings gradually fell into ruin, leaving only foundations and stone chimneys, gaunt against the sky, to recall the brief five years in which Fort Lancaster kept watch over the Pecos crossing. The ruins are encompassed within a Crockett County historic site adjacent to U.S. Highway 290 about ten miles east of Sheffield.

SOURCES: Crimmins, ed., "Mansfield's Report"; Frazer, *Forts of the West*; Holden, "Frontier Defense"; Prucha, *Guide*.

BACHELOR OFFICERS' QUARTERS, FORT LANCASTER

It is sundown and the flag is being lowered. Supper is ready for the four officers who live here and is being served in the shadow of the building. The small room at the far right next to the kitchen is the privy, and the table is where meat is butchered.

FORT RICHARDSON

Military planners conceived of Fort Richardson as the northern anchor of the new chain of forts that would guard the western edge of Texas settlement in the years after the Civil War. It would be a strongly garrisoned post, strategically positioned to ward off the parties of Kiowa and Comanche warriors that for generations had splashed across the Red River to raid the Texas and Mexican frontiers. After months of confusion over where to build, Fort Richardson finally began to take shape late in 1867 on the south bank of Lost Creek, a tributary of the Trinity River.

From the soldier's viewpoint, Fort Richardson had its attractions. Stunted pecans, scrub oak, and mesquite relieved the monotony of the range lands stretching to the horizon in all directions. Antelope, deer, wild turkey, prairie chicken, and duck abounded, and in the winter months buffalo could be had by riding thirty or forty miles to the north. Lost Creek supported few fish, but the Brazos, thirty miles to the west, teemed with catfish, drum, and buffalo fish, while turtles beyond counting swarmed in every stream. Constant breezes moderated the fierce summer heat, and winter brought little snow or severe cold.

Settlers provided varied society. Some five hundred people lived in the hamlet of Jacksboro, only half a mile north of the parade ground, and bold ranchers willing to risk their scalps against the hope of gain ran cattle in scattered isolation across the rich grasslands.

Not that the troopers found nothing to grouse about. The country crawled with centipedes, scorpions, and tarantulas, and no recess of home or clothing could be counted free of them. Copperheads, moccasins, puff adders, and rattlesnakes required constant wariness. In the winter snowless "northers" plunged temperatures to subzero levels for several days at a time, and in the summer violent thunderstorms tore across the land, wrecking property and transforming dry streambeds into roaring torrents that paralyzed travel. And, besides, the fort itself scarcely provided comfortable accommodations.

The post that rose from the banks of Lost Creek turned out to be a curious mixture of good solid structures of locally quarried sandstone and rude habitations of twisted pecan or cottonwood "pickets," planted upright like a stockade and chinked with plaster. Even more curious, except for the hospital, the substantial buildings sheltered quartermaster and commissary stores, while the picket shacks housed the garrison. Badly crowded, badly ventilated, badly heated, badly deteriorating from the day of completion, the picket barracks drew the ire of the surgeon, who branded them in every way unhealthful. The soldiers slept on straw-filled mattresses laid on double-decked wooden bunks, four feet wide, two men on each deck. They bathed in a deep hole of Lost Creek in summer; winter sanitation can be imagined.

Even the officers had cause for complaint. Half the officers' line consisted of reasonably comfortable frame buildings, with doors and windows hauled from the supply depot at San Antonio; but the other half were of the same picket construction the enlisted men endured.

And then there was Sudsville, a motley collection of frame and picket shacks, log huts, and tents where lived the laundresses and married enlisted men.

By contrast, the hospital and quartermaster and commissary storehouses were truly imposing and much admired. The two storehouses had been built on line at the east edge of the parade ground, with a twenty-foot gap between them intended to be connected by an ornate arch that would form the entrance to the post. Before the arch could be inserted, however, someone with a need for more space filled the gap with an unsightly wooden room and converted the two buildings into one. And thus it remained ever after.

Fort Richardson's era of greatest activity and significance began in 1871, when the Fourth Cavalry replaced the Sixth. To the north, beyond the Red River, the

Kiowas and Comanches had recently been settled on the Fort Sill Reservation, and gentle Quaker agents had arrived to put into effect President Grant's new Peace Policy. The Indians drew rations and other gifts at Fort Sill while continuing to kill and plunder along the Texas frontier. The Peace Policy barred the Sixth Cavalry from pursuing the raiders across the Red River into their "City of Refuge," and anyway the Sixth was not a particularly energetic outfit. The Fourth, however, followed Ranald S. Mackenzie, and he had no intention of sitting quietly at his desk in the Fort Richardson post headquarters.

Among those who came with Mackenzie was a young officer named Robert G. Carter, newly graduated from West Point, newly married en route to his first station, and accompanied by his bride. In later years Carter was a pompous, vain, and boastful old man, but as a young subaltern he seems to have been competent, respected by his men, and valued by his colonel. He remembered his service at Fort Richardson in vivid detail.

He remembered how badly overcrowded the fort was, with almost three hundred officers and men in space intended for less than half that many, how even the officers and their families had to double up in the quarters along officers' row. Some eased the press by erecting tents behind the houses for kitchens. Carter and his wife went a step further. They fitted together a whole complex of tents at the east end of officers' row and set up housekeeping entirely under canvas.

Neither the lieutenant nor his wife ever forgot a wild night in November 1872. A norther swept down on the fort. A detachment of soldiers holding down the guy ropes and picket pins of the Carter domicile prevented the tents from blowing away while, inside, the post surgeon assisted in the birth of an infant daughter, the couple's first child.

The Carters remembered the good times more than the bad—the theatricals, which usually turned out less than triumphantly; and the "hops," which were always successful, with the officers resplendent in blue and gold,

the ladies in the best that could be mustered on the frontier, the regimental band inviting all to the dance, and tables heavy with turkey, venison, bear, ham, smoked buffalo, quail, canned oysters, preserves, and *real* mince pies made from *real* apples hauled from Arkansas by bull train. Similar repasts graced other occasions, such as the Christmas party arranged around a huge centerpiece of frosted pastry adorned with pink letters: "Troop C, Fourth Cavalry, Christmas 1872, Welcome!"

Everyone had a pet—dogs, cats, pigs, even a young buffalo—but best remembered was the pet nanny goat of Captain Wilcox's daughter Mary. It dominated garrison life, ruining property, fouling the environment, and terrorizing youngsters. Then one day the beast antagonized Dr. Hammond, a relic of a quarter of a century of medical service, benign and mild-mannered beneath flowing white beard and hair but with legendary capacity for soft-spoken yet powerfully expressive profanity. He left open the door to his laboratory, a retreat full of test tubes, retorts, beakers, and sundry chemicals and other fluids. In walked the goat and devastated the place. Next day Mary's nanny disappeared. Weeks of search, fortified by a reward, turned up no trace of the animal, and no one ever knew her fate. Years later, Hammond confessed to Carter: "I gave her a pound, more or less, of Paris Green, and had her secretly buried."

Such adventures of garrison life formed a backdrop for the hard field service required by Colonel Mackenzie's unrelenting drive. He could not cross the Red River onto the Indian reservation, but he could campaign elsewhere, and he did, even as far distant as the Staked Plains. There in September 1872 he won a stunning victory over Comanches at the Battle of McClellan Creek.

When Mackenzie came to Fort Richardson, Washington officials had not admitted that Indian depredations in Texas were more than a Texan ploy to get federal troops out of the interior of the state, where their Reconstruction duties antagonized the citizens. Even the Army's commanding general, acerbic old William Tecumseh

PICKET HOUSES, FORT RICHARDSON

During the first winter these temporary quarters were built for the men. The fire inside gives some warmth but also dries the mud keeping out the drafts between the poles, requiring constant maintenance.

COMMISSARY WAREHOUSE, FORT RICHARDSON

Originally this was to be the grand entrance gate to the fort, but a more convenient road was used instead.
The entrance was enclosed (wooden structure) for the use of the quartermaster.

Sherman, doubted the truth of settlers' complaints of Kiowa-Comanche raids from the reservation sanctuary, so he set forth to see for himself.

Unknown to Sherman as he approached Fort Richardson in May 1871, a Kiowa war party lay in ambush on Salt Creek prairie, west of the fort. Present were some of the most prominent Kiowa leaders, including Satanta, Big Tree, Satank, and Big Bow. As they made ready to fall on the general's ambulance with its little cavalry escort, the medicine man Mamanti spoke up. Wait, he said, let this train pass, for another, richer train would soon be along. The prophecy proved correct. Shortly, ten freight wagons appeared. The warriors swarmed to the attack. Five whites escaped, but the rest fell under the onslaught. The raiders mutilated the corpses, plundered and burned the wagons, and rode off with forty-one mules. That night, as Sherman listened to the complaints of the Jacksboro citizens, a badly wounded Tom Brazeale staggered into the post hospital with his tale of the massacre.

Sherman's doubts instantly vanished. Mackenzie mounted his regiment and set off in pursuit. A grimly determined general-in-chief, oblivious to how close he had come to losing his own scalp, set off for the Fort Sill refuge of the Kiowas and Comanches. A few weeks later two of the culprits, Satanta and Big Tree, arrived at Fort Richardson from Fort Sill in chains and under heavy guard. A third chief, old Satank, had been shot and killed en route while trying to escape. A cowboy jury at Jacksboro convicted the two Indians of murder, and the judge sentenced them to be hanged. But federal officials persuaded the Reconstruction governor of Texas to commute the sentences to life imprisonment, and two years later Satanta and Big Tree were sent back to their people.

Fort Richardson continued to play a vital role in the frontier defenses of Texas as long as the Kiowas and Comanches remained unconquered. At the conclusion of the Red River War of 1874–1875, in which Mackenzie and his regiment campaigned with great distinction, they surrendered for the last time. Back to the Huntsville penitentiary went Satanta and Big Tree. Here in 1878 a despairing Satanta flung himself from an upper window to his death. In this same year, the northern flank of the Texas frontier finally secure, the last troops marched away from Fort Richardson.

Today a state historical reserve, Fort Richardson stands on the southern edge of Jacksboro and is administered by the Jack County Historical Society. Seven buildings remain. The hospital building houses a museum.

SOURCES: Billings, *Report on Barracks* and *Report on Hygiene*; Carter, *On the Border*; Frazer, *Forts of the West*; McConnell, *Five Years*; Prucha, *Guide*; Richardson, *Comanche Barrier* and *Frontier of Northwest Texas*; Wallace, *Mackenzie*; Whisenhunt, *Fort Richardson*.

FORT GRIFFIN

To bluff, chunky Lieutenant Colonel Samuel D. Sturgis fell responsibility for the next link south of Fort Richardson in the chain of Texas frontier forts laid out after the Civil War. Veteran of the Mexican War and a decade of frontier experience, Sturgis led four troops of the Sixth U.S. Cavalry into old Fort Belknap in the spring of 1867.

He did not like the place. The water tasted terrible, the dilapidated and comfortless buildings put up back in the 1850s were poorly situated for defense, and the once thriving town of Fort Belknap lay deserted, a casualty of Indian raids during the war years.

So Sturgis sent an officer to look for another site. He found it about forty miles to the southwest, where the Clear Fork of the Brazos River made a sweeping turn from south to east in its flow toward the main channel of the Brazos. In midsummer of 1867, to the joy of the handful of cattlemen who had ventured back into the area, Sturgis marched most of his cavalrymen to this place. They pitched camp on a gently sloping plateau some five hundred feet above the valley floor. Here, on "Government Hill," Fort Griffin began to take shape.

Like the other frontier forts, Griffin was to be a post of durability and comfort, and the quartermaster down in San Antonio freighted in a steam sawmill, door and window frames, a crew of civilian "mechanics," and plenty of construction tools. Up went rude temporary structures to shelter the garrison while fine edifices of stone were built.

They were never built, and when the last troops marched away fourteen years later many of these same makeshift habitations still served. True, the log cabin moved from an abandoned ranch to house the commanding officer had been replaced by a commodious two-story frame dwelling, and officers' row took on more ample and comfortable proportions. But the enlisted men lived throughout in frame huts measuring thirteen by eight by six feet. There were forty of them, arranged in four rows.

The surgeon called them "shanties" and, with six men crowded into each, blamed them in part for the high incidence of dysentery and fever. The hospital was also a log building moved from an old ranch. It had a dirt roof, leaned badly, and was in such rundown shape by 1870 that strips of canvas had to be tacked up to protect the medical stores from falling dirt and leaking water. Over the years the hospital grew, as other "temporary" buildings were thrown together and connected to it. Storehouses, guardhouse, offices, and other structures recorded a similar history of deterioration and improvisation.

The discomforts of Fort Griffin, especially during the period when the men labored on the officers' quarters to the neglect of their own, scarcely promoted good morale. And, aggravating conditions, the fort turned out to be so strategically located that, during the peak Indian hostilities of the early 1870s, it housed an unusually strong garrison of about three hundred men, both infantry and cavalry. The soldiers packed themselves into the little huts and spilled over into tents.

They vented their frustrations on "the Flat," where on two sides of a dusty street leading from the base of Government Hill to the timber-fringed river the town of Fort Griffin grew into one of the most notorious of the "hog ranches" that cursed virtually every Army post in the West. The saloons and brothels of the Flat catered to every human appetite and, sustained by the big garrison on the hill, attracted adventurers, desperadoes, outlaws of every persuasion, "soiled doves" by the score, and all sorts of depraved outpourings from more civilized realms.

From 1867 until the final conquest of the Kiowas and Comanches, Indian raiders preoccupied the Fort Griffin garrison. Detachments of cavalry laced the mesquite-carpeted hills and ridges rolling off to the west and worked their way up the pleasantly wooded valleys of the various forks of the Brazos flowing down from the Staked Plains. Usually the raiding parties from the reservation

BAKERY, FORT GRIFFIN

The bread for the day has been baking since before dawn and is now being delivered to the mess halls in time for breakfast. In the background are the commanding officer's quarters and the post adjutant's office.

42

FOUR-MAN BARRACKS, FORT GRIFFIN

This was an unsuccessful experiment in barracks housing because each four-man barracks maintained a fireplace in this area where wood for fuel was scarce. Quarters were cramped and often resulted in bedding catching fire, causing the place to burn down. Note the mess hall in the background.

43

north of the Red River easily kept clear of the patrols and plundered and killed the entire length of the frontier to the Rio Grande.

One of the most brutal attacks occurred on a warm June Sunday in 1872 at a farm sixteen miles down the river from Fort Griffin. White Horse, a leading Kiowa warrior, and five other men had ridden into Texas to seek revenge for the death of White Horse's brother in an earlier raid. Abel Lee sat peacefully on his front porch reading a newspaper when a bullet from White Horse's rifle smashed into his chest. Inside, Mrs. Lee screamed and with the children tried to escape through the back door. An arrow buried itself between her shoulder blades. In the vegetable garden outside, another arrow dropped fourteen-year-old Frances. Susanna, Millie, and John, ages seventeen, nine, and six, fell captive to the Kiowas. After scalping and mutilating the slain settlers, the Indians loaded the prisoners on their ponies and rode back to the reservation. That night a storm filled the Clear Fork, preventing troops from Fort Griffin from even getting across the river to the Lee ranch. Neighbors buried the victims. Not until more than a year later did the Indian agent at Fort Sill secure the release of the Lee children.

Not that the Fort Griffin soldiers failed altogether in confronting the Kiowas and Comanches. In 1868 Captain Adna R. Chaffee, one day to become the nation's top soldier, won a signal victory over Comanches. Elements of the Fort Griffin command participated in Colonel Ranald S. Mackenzie's expedition to the Staked Plains in 1871, and in 1872 Mackenzie brought the Comanche captives seized in the Battle of McClellan Creek to Fort Griffin. In the climactic Red River War of 1874–1875, one of the five striking columns that converged on the Staked Plains was based at Griffin. And early in 1874, a pursuing force out of Griffin, led by Lieutenant Colonel George P. Buell, inflicted a severe defeat on Comanches at Double Mountain, west of the fort.

Such success as the Griffin troops could claim sprang in part from a remarkable unit of Tonkawa Indian scouts based at the fort. Originally from Texas, the Tonkawas had been moved to Indian Territory before the Civil War. But in 1862 neighboring groups, possibly incensed by the cannibalistic habits of which the Tonkawas were accused, wiped out half the tribe. The survivors fled back to Texas. Now, rationed by the U.S. Army, the men served as scouts while their families lived under the protection of the fort. No visit to Fort Griffin was complete without a tour of the Tonkawa village. At Double Mountain, the Tonkawas fought with special skill and valor under command of Lieutenant Richard H. Pratt, who later achieved fame as founder and superintendent of the Carlisle Indian School.

Pratt served at Fort Griffin in 1873–1874, when elements of the Tenth Cavalry—black troopers with white officers—made up the mounted contingent. Almost at once Pratt was placed in charge of the Tonkawa scout detachment. He found them demoralized by the drink that flowed so freely on the Flat. Instituting novel but effective measures, he brought the problem under control, obtained convictions of whiskey sellers, and made the Tonkawas into first-rate scouts and trailers.

Pratt was also a sportsman, and he reveled in the abundance of game that endowed the Fort Griffin country. Routinely officers felled buffalo, deer, wild turkeys, and smaller animals and birds that varied the monotonous army diet. On one expedition Pratt killed six deer in one day. On another he discovered that the deep pools, or "lakelets," that marked the course of the Clear Fork teemed with huge bass. Back at the fort he organized a fishing expedition. Taking a spring wagon manned by Captain Philip L. Lee's noted black cook, Pratt and a band of fellow officers headed back up the Clear Fork. All enjoyed fine success and in the evening assembled for a feast—only to find that the cook had failed to load any utensils on the wagon. Improvisation won out, however, with thin flat stones serving as frying pans and minnow buckets as coffee pots.

Buffalo abounded, and scouting parties usually brought back choice hams, tongues, and humps to distribute among the garrison. So profuse were buffalo that they were even known to stampede across the Fort Griffin parade ground itself. Officers recalled one such occasion when a Tenth Cavalry lieutenant ran out of his quarters and tried to bring down a buffalo with only his saber. The beast was last seen galloping into the distance with the saber stuck securely in its side.

Paradoxically, as the military and Indian phases of Fort Griffin's history began to wane, other historical themes assumed a prominence that made the Fort Griffin country almost a microcosm of the westward movement. They took on this significance precisely because the army and the Indian no longer contended for this part of the frontier. After the Red River War of 1874–1875, only an occasional marauding party rode down the frontier line from the reservation. Most of the Kiowas and Comanches stayed north of the Red River, and the great sweep of plains at the foot of the caprock, and the Staked Plains above it, knew an unprecedented security.

As a result the Fort Griffin country boomed. The fort itself declined to a one-company post. But the town doubled in population, to about a thousand, and through the late 1870s it was the economic, commercial, and social center of a vast area of northwestern Texas. Ranchers spread up and down the Clear Fork and the other streams. The Western Trail all but supplanted the Chisholm Trail, overrun by the settlers' frontier to the east, as the busiest cattle trail from South Texas to the Kansas and Nebraska railroads. And most important of all, Fort Griffin became the base and outfitting point for the swarms of hide hunters that descended on the buffalo grazing the grasslands to the west. In about five years they decimated the southern herds of some five million animals. At Fort Griffin they bought their ammunition, food, and other supplies, and to Fort Griffin they hauled their hides for shipment to eastern tanneries.

Thus Fort Griffin's stores, hotels, restaurants, saloons, and bawdy houses teemed with ranchmen, trail drivers, buffalo hunters, and all the parasites that lived off them. Cattle rustlers, horse thieves, and desperadoes flocked to the great hide entrepôt of the Texas frontier, and in their wake came lawmen, Texas Rangers, and homegrown vigilantes. The Flat rocked with homicide, mayhem, larceny, and other varieties of lawlessness, as well as the riotous fun-making of men come in for a night on the town.

Then, abruptly, it ended. The Indians had been conquered and confined to their reservations. The southern herds of buffalo had dwindled to the verge of extinction. The Texas and Pacific Railroad bypassed Griffin to the south. On May 31, 1881, Company A, Twenty-second Infantry, lowered the national colors from the flagstaff in the center of the Fort Griffin parade ground and marched off for another station. A few stubborn holdouts remained on the Flat, together with the hapless Tonkawas, now deserted by their military protectors. In 1884 the Indian Bureau moved the Tonkawas back to Indian Territory.

Fort Griffin State Park contains the stone remains of a few military structures. The Flat is in private ownership. The site is located on U.S. Highway 283 about fifteen miles north of Albany.

SOURCES: Billings, *Report on Barracks* and *Report on Hygiene*; Carter, *On the Border*; Frazer, *Forts of the West*; Prucha, *Guide*; Richardson, *Comanche Barrier* and *Frontier of Northwest Texas*; Rister, *Fort Griffin*; Wallace, *Mackenzie*.

(following page)
COMMANDING OFFICER'S QUARTERS, FORT GRIFFIN
This may have been a fort to some, but to the families of the officers it was home, where friends visited and children played. In the background is the hospital.

COMMANDING OFFICER'S QUARTERS
FORT GRIFFIN

OFFICERS' ROW, FORT GRIFFIN

What a strange assortment of buildings for a fort! Six houses were found in the area, dismantled, carried by
wagons to the fort, and rebuilt for officers' quarters. Note the typical construction of the post flagpole.

47

FORT CONCHO

Fort Concho came to life because prewar Fort Chadbourne's water had failed and another site had to be found. Major John P. Hatch fixed on the forks of the Concho, thirty-five miles to the south. With five troops of the Fourth U.S. Cavalry, he camped here early in December 1867. First named Camp Hatch, then Camp Kelly, then Fort Griffin, the new link in the outer ring of frontier defenses finally acquired its permanent label in February 1868.

Hatch could scarcely have chosen a more strategic location. Several east-west travel routes, including the San Antonio–El Paso "Upper Road" and the old Butterfield Trail, converged here to avoid the Staked Plains on the north and a forbidding desert on the south. Also, the Goodnight–Loving Trail bore countless herds of longhorns through the Concho country to the Pecos and on to rich ranges and markets in New Mexico. And down from the north swept the Great Comanche War Trail, one branch pointing south and west to the Big Bend and Mexico, the other closely hugging the frontier of settlement directly southward. Fort Concho held the very center of the outer cordon of forts and was the base from which the military line projected westward to El Paso.

Major Hatch could claim little credit for the fine fort that rose from the south bank of the Concho just below its forks. The troops called him "Dobe" Hatch because of his partiality to adobe as a building material. But his successor preferred stone, locally plentiful, and the substantial buildings he began to construct in February 1868 eventually formed one of the best and most comfortable posts in Texas. True, the woodwork left something to be desired. The lumber, noted the surgeon, came from a "peculiarly intractable" species of pecan growing in the Concho Valley and was characterized by "twisting, curling, and shrinking." "Ventilation and light," he observed drily, "thanks to shrinking windows and doors, are abundantly supplied."

Like most other frontier forts, Concho did not look like a conventional military station. The young officer ordered here would be badly disappointed, remarked the surgeon, if "his experience has taught him that the isolated post among merciless foes should be what it is named, a *fort*." It consisted of an officers' row facing enlisted men's barracks across a spacious parade ground, with guardhouse, hospital, offices, and storehouses spotted on either end and stables and corrals behind—all solidly built of stone. Curiously and conspicuously, no flagstaff rose from the center of the parade ground, as a suitable pole was not to be had closer than Fredericksburg. General Sherman and other visitors commented sourly on the deficiency, but not until 1874 did an embarrassed post commander overcome the obstacles and give Concho the symbol of its military identity.

Despite the comforts of the stone buildings, people sent to Concho found it a dreary place. Except for the river valley, it was set in a treeless waste, sprinkled with mesquite and everywhere pocked with "dog towns" whose warrens harbored rattlesnakes as well as prairie dogs. Centipedes, tarantulas, and scorpions infested every likely retreat. One officer reached for his towel only to have a seven-inch centipede fall from it onto his hand and leave him with a painful bite. And of course the military community assigned the top spot on the list of venomous denizens of the neighborhood to the regular attacks of Kiowa and Comanche war parties.

The climate was abominable—howling, freezing winter northers; blasting summer heat with prolonged droughts and driving dust storms; rain that came all at once, in torrents that flooded the streams or hail that damaged buildings and killed exposed stock. While still under canvas in 1868, for example, the troops endured a hailstorm that beat down every tent, stampeded all the cavalry horses, killed most of the garrison's poultry, and left two inches of ice on the parade ground. In 1870 another storm caught Major Henry C. Merriam and party camped at the head of the Middle Concho; the river rose suddenly during the night and swept away the entire camp, including the major's wife, their child, the child's nurse, three soldiers, and his carriage and teams.

One offsetting advantage was abundant game. Few posts afforded such a sportsman's paradise. Deer, antelope, wild turkey, quail, teal, and peccary ranged the prairies in profusion, while bass and catfish even to seventy-five pounds stocked the streams. In winter the great southern herds of buffalo dropped southward to the Concho country.

The buffalo gave more than local importance to the town of Saint Angela, the "hog ranch" across the river from the post. Like the Flat at Fort Griffin, this raucous hamlet catered to the appetites of the soldiery while also serving as an outfitting point for buffalo hide hunters. The officers and their wives thought badly of their neighboring community, although in 1871 the post chaplain ventured across the river to deliver its first sermon. The surgeon was sure that this occasion marked "the first time that the name of the deity was ever publicly used in reverence in that place." In 1881, when a storm lifted the North Concho fifteen feet in ten minutes, a later chaplain smugly recorded that it "swept away several drinking saloons & miserable lodging places of outside camp-followers," together, added the surgeon, with "all houses, stores, etc. on or near the river bank." But in the end Saint Angela proved more enduring than Fort Concho, eventually swallowing the post and evolving into the thriving city of San Angelo.

Fort Concho's garrison scouted the Concho country in an effort to turn aside the Indian raiding parties from the north and also participated in the larger operations against these Indians, including Ranald S. Mackenzie's campaigns and the Red River War of 1874–1875. For much of the 1870s these men of Concho were in whole or part black troops—the famed "buffalo soldiers." For part of this time the fort served as regimental headquarters of the Tenth Cavalry, Colonel Benjamin H. Grierson commanding.

Although Grierson's name is intimately linked to Fort Concho, perhaps a more significant association is that of William Rufus Shafter, lieutenant-colonel of the black Twenty-fourth Infantry. Coarse, profane, hard-driving taskmaster, strict disciplinarian, unpopular with his officers, a barely concealed racist who nevertheless stood up for his black troops and led them effectively, Shafter campaigned so tirelessly across the vast hostile terrain of West Texas that he became known as "Pecos Bill." His field record is all the more remarkable because he was a huge man—"a sort of human fortress in blue coat and flannel shirt," William Randolph Hearst would later describe him. Neither horse nor saddle bore his ample frame comfortably or effectively, but that did not deter him.

Shafter first commanded Fort Concho in 1870, but it was an expedition he led forth from Concho in 1875 that contributed most memorably to the opening of West Texas. Ordered to sweep the Staked Plains free of Indian raiders, he marched out of Concho with a formidable command of nine companies of cavalry and infantry, sixty-five wagons, seven hundred pack mules, and a large beef herd, established a supply base on the upper Brazos River, and then with his cavalry plunged into the "dreaded Sahara of North America."

For six months this dogged officer who by all anatomical standards should have sat out his career at a desk kept his columns on the trail of the elusive foe. Wrote one officer to his wife: "I think that our horses will go to the devil very fast at the rate Col. Shafter charges the whole command after everything. I do not think you would like to scout with Colonel Shafter." And this at a time when the big colonel was so plagued by varicose veins that he rode day after day with one leg strapped to his horse's neck and had to be helped to mount and dismount.

SCHOOL-LIBRARY-CHURCH, FORT CONCHO

It is Easter Sunday, and all are arrayed in their best clothes for church service. This building also served as school and library. In the background at left is officers' row, and at right is the parade ground with barracks beyond. Note the entrance to the storm cellar to the left of the church.

Hospital
Fort Concho

HOSPITAL, FORT CONCHO

The center section housed the reception room and doctor's office on the first floor and the doctor's living quarters on the second floor. The wings were the wards, with the end room on the right as a surgery room. The little house in the background at right is the morgue. On the left is post headquarters.

By the time he gave up the chase, Shafter had covered and described the Staked Plains from the caprock on the east to the Pecos River on the west, from the Monahans Sands on the south almost to the Canadian River on the north. This great expanse of grassland stood revealed in all its inviting richness. And so Shafter reported to a world hitherto ignorant of and intimidated by this immense dry table. The following summer, 1876, Charles Goodnight and the vanguard of the cattlemen moved onto the Staked Plains.

The Red River War marked the final conquest of the Kiowas and Comanches. After 1875, as Goodnight's first herds on the Staked Plains suggested, the danger of Kiowa and Comanche raids receded. Fort Concho persisted through the 1880s as its neighbor, Saint Angela, matured into a marketing center for cattle ranchers rather than buffalo hunters. In 1889 the flag came down as the Army pulled out, but it was destined to rise again as Fort Concho took on a new role as one of the best preserved and restored frontier forts in the West. Ironically, given the historic animosity between town and post, Fort Concho is owned and proudly exhibited by the City of San Angelo.

SOURCES: Billings, *Report on Barracks* and *Report on Hygiene*; Frazer, *Forts of the West*; Green, *Dancing*; Haley, *Fort Concho*; Prucha, *Guide*.

FORT DAVIS

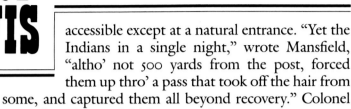

In 1854 General Persifor Smith, commanding the Department of Texas, decided that military protection of the Trans-Pecos travel routes could be delayed no longer. Apache and Comanche raiders constantly threatened mail, freight, and emigrant traffic on the Upper and Lower Roads and all too often succeeded in waylaying a mail coach or over-running a train. With the inner and outer rings of forts in place along the frontier of settlement, Smith set forth in the autumn of 1854 to extend the Texas defense system westward to El Paso. On October 23, roughly midway between the Pecos and El Paso, he directed Lieutenant Colonel Washington Seawell and six companies of the Eighth U.S. Infantry to erect a new fort, which he named in honor of the Secretary of War, Jefferson Davis.

The site selected combined the advantages of a strategic location with an appealing setting. Situated on the eastern edge of the Limpia Mountains (which promptly became the Davis Mountains), Fort Davis commanded some of the most vulnerable stretches of the Lower Road as well as the principal trails of Comanches and Apaches from their northern ranges to favored raiding targets in Mexico.

At General Smith's direction, the fort was built in a pretty box canyon opening on a rolling plain studded with rocky peaks and mesas. Limpia Creek provided clear fresh water, and a spring at the canyon's mouth irrigated a bounteous vegetable garden. The Davis Mountains, a grassy, timbered oasis rising from the forbidding Trans-Pecos wastes, yielded ample lumber, teemed with game animals, and offered splendid scenery as well. The climate was the finest in Texas—cool in summer, mild in winter.

However picturesque the dark rock turrets and boulder-strewn slopes of the canyon, it hardly made a good site for a fort deep in the Indian country. When Colonel J. K. F. Mansfield inspected Fort Davis in 1856, the beef contractor had just lost his entire herd. The cattle had been corraled on a mountain ledge thought in-accessible except at a natural entrance. "Yet the Indians in a single night," wrote Mansfield, "altho' not 500 yards from the post, forced them up thro' a pass that took off the hair from some, and captured them all beyond recovery." Colonel Seawell told Mansfield he wanted to move the post out on the flat near the spring. But one did not lightly over-ride decisions made by a commanding general. In the canyon it remained—a ramshackle assortment of some sixty jacales of pine slabs with thatched roofs, adobe boxes covered with canvas, and, finally, six stone barracks with grass roofs and flagstone floors. Except for the barracks, the structures quickly went to ruin as the slabs warped and rotted and the other shoddy materials deteriorated similarly.

Fort Davis brought a military presence to the Trans-Pecos and a way station to the long westward reach of the San Antonio–El Paso Road. It afforded some protection to travelers and caused the Indians to exercise a bit more care in their passage through the country. But infantrymen armed with cumbersome muskets and mounted on mules were scarcely a match for the swift-riding warriors. Gamely the soldiers patrolled the road and tried to catch Indian war parties, but rarely did they overtake the enemy. As Colonel Mansfield remarked of one such expedition, a young lieutenant's two-hundred-mile chase, "as a matter of course his pursuit was a failure."

As at most other Texas outposts, Southern troops held Fort Davis for a time during the Civil War. They had no more success than their blueclad predecessors in contending with Indians. In August 1861, in fact, Lieutenant Reuben E. Mays and fourteen horsemen out of Fort Davis rode into an Apache ambush from which not one escaped. After the failure of the Confederate invasion of New Mexico, the Texans pulled out and Fort Davis lay deserted for the rest of the war.

On June 29, 1867, Lieutenant Colonel Wesley Merritt and four troops of the Ninth U.S. Cavalry bivouacked

CHAPEL AND POST HEADQUARTERS, FORT DAVIS

This is the day the trial begins for Lieutenant Henry Flipper. It is held in the chapel, and school has been
canceled, much to the delight of the children. The judge advocate stands waiting for the principals to arrive.
Walking toward the chapel are Lieutenant Flipper and his attorney. Colonel Shafter is approaching from post headquarters.

54

COMMANDING OFFICER'S QUARTERS, FORT DAVIS

The piano that Colonel Grierson purchased back East has arrived. The colonel was a music teacher before the Civil War, and all of his children are musically talented. There will be a grand concert from their porch tonight to entertain the whole post.

55

at Fort Davis, their mission to reactivate the fort as part of the postwar defense system. They found the old fort in the canyon wrecked and partly burned. This was not a disappointment, for Merritt promptly decided to build a fine stone post such as Seawell had envisioned near the spring outside the canyon. Across the mouth of the canyon stretched officers' row, ultimately nineteen residences of stone and adobe fronting a five-hundred-foot parade ground and facing commodious barracks with deep porches. Other buildings rose at both ends of the parade ground and, together with the corrals, behind the barracks. Over the next two decades, the post on the flat evolved into an installation surpassing even the fondest dreams of Colonel Seawell. As early as 1870 the surgeon could write: "Fort Davis, by reason of its delightful climate, its healthfulness and comfortable quarters, is one of the most desirable posts on the Texas frontier, and the surrounding country may be called grand and picturesque."

Colonel Merritt and his black troopers launched a long and intimate association between Fort Davis and the "buffalo soldiers." Between 1867 and 1881, all four black regiments—the Ninth and Tenth Cavalry and the Twenty-fourth and Twenty-fifth Infantry—did duty at Davis. They patrolled the Lower Road both east and west, provided escorts for freight trains and mail coaches, and endured some of the most punishing campaigns in frontier history across the great tangle of parched mountain-and-desert terrain extending from the Guadalupe Mountains on the north to the canyons of the Rio Grande's Big Bend on the south. Faced with searing discrimination both in and out of the Army, the blacks at first justified the skepticism that greeted their incorporation into the regular Army. But over the years low desertion rates and high reenlistment rates filled the four regiments with veterans, and the buffalo soldiers eventually could point proudly to an outstanding record of frontier service.

Fort Davis was the setting in 1881 for one of the most publicized episodes of discrimination against blacks. The perpetrator was none other than "Pecos Bill" Shafter, the same big officer who had explored the Staked Plains in 1875 and compiled such a bright record as an officer of black troops. The victim was Lieutenant Henry O. Flipper, the first black graduate of West Point and an officer of the Tenth Cavalry. As post quartermaster at Fort Davis, Flipper was undoubtedly guilty of loose fiscal practices. But Shafter, then commanding the post, brought him before a court-martial on charges of embezzlement. The celebrated trial took place in a makeshift courtroom in the post chapel. The verdict: not guilty of embezzlement but guilty of conduct unbecoming an officer and a gentleman. The sentence: dismissal from the Army. On the basis of the evidence, no white officer would have been made to pay such a penalty, or even convicted; and there can be little question that, in the eyes of Shafter, the court, and the reviewing authority, Flipper's real offense was to taint the racial purity of the U.S. Army officer corps. Flipper went on to a long and distinguished career as a mining engineer.

Another officer of black troops whose name is firmly linked to Fort Davis was Colonel Benjamin H. Grierson. He was an unlikely soldier. An Illinois music teacher caught up in the Civil War, he found himself in the cavalry despite a childhood encounter with a horse that left his jaw so disfigured that he wore an enormous beard to conceal it. Incongruously, this gentle, kindly man whose interests focused on his family and his music ended the war a major general and the hero of "Grierson's Raid" through the heart of Confederate Mississippi. A regular Army commission followed in 1866, and for the next quarter-century he commanded the Tenth Cavalry. Some thought him too easygoing and benevolent to command very effectively. He found it hard to be strict with his black troopers, just as he found it hard to war against Indians whom he believed unjustly treated.

When he had to war, though, he could, as he proved in the Victorio outbreak of 1879–1880, which occurred while he made his headquarters at Fort Davis. Victorio and his Apache followers had struck terror through three states and much of northern Mexico and had outwitted or outfought the military forces of two nations. Grierson won not by giving chase but by seizing and holding the widely scattered water holes of West Texas. The test came at Tinaja de las Palmas, a watering place in barren Quitman Canyon, on July 30, 1880. Grierson himself and his teenage son Robert happened to be behind the rude defenses when Victorio rode against them. The defenders held, and soon fresh buffalo soldiers charged into the attacking Indians, "& golly," young Robert wrote in his diary, "you ought to've seen 'em turn tail & strike for the hills." By denying vital water to the Apaches, Grierson forced them back into Mexico and kept them there until Mexican troops won a stunning victory in which Victorio was killed.

Victorio's death marked the close of Indian warfare in West Texas. The ranges safe, cattlemen ventured across the Pecos and onto the rich grasses of the Davis Mountains. No longer needed, Fort Davis was finally abandoned in 1891. Across the road from the fort as the last infantrymen marched away, a newly arrived cattleman was at work on his new home. Brigadier General Benjamin H. Grierson, U.S. Army Retired, had come back to Fort Davis to begin life as a rancher.

Today Fort Davis is a national historic site and has been expertly restored by the National Park Service. In the center of officers' row, the commanding officer's quarters has been recreated as "Grierson House" and furnished as it would have appeared when the Griersons lived there and the tall, bearded colonel passed quiet summer evenings playing the violin on the front veranda.

SOURCES: Billings, *Report on Barracks* and *Report on Hygiene*; Frazer, *Forts of the West*; Prucha, *Guide*; Scobee, *Fort Davis*.

FORT BLISS

Few western outposts traced a more erratic history than Fort Bliss. In its first half-century it occupied no less than six locations, succumbed twice to abandonment, bore three official names, and wavered in its allegiance between the Department of New Mexico and the Department of Texas, reporting sometimes northward to Santa Fe, other times eastward to San Antonio. Yet Fort Bliss survived and lives on as one of the nation's most important Army bases.

In its first incarnation, 1849–1851, Fort Bliss bore the designation "Post Opposite El Paso del Norte." Several thousand citizens lived in the Mexican city on the south bank of the Rio Grande that later, with the rise of the American El Paso on the Texas side of the river, took the name Ciudad Juárez. Since the earliest Spanish colonists, the "Pass of the North" had been an important place. Here the Rio Grande cut through barren brown mountains and swung abruptly to the east to water a sandy desert plain as it made its way toward the Gulf of Mexico. Here as elsewhere in the Southwest the Apache menace was pervasive. Here the north-south Chihuahua Trail, for more than two centuries a major commercial artery linking northern Mexico with remote Santa Fe, intersected the newer mail and emigrant roads across the Southwest to California.

Dramatizing the fort's crossroads location, the first garrison, six companies of the Third U.S. Infantry under Major Jefferson Van Horne, escorted the military surveyors who pioneered the Lower Road across West Texas. They ended their summer-long trek through the hot, thirsty deserts from San Antonio in September 1849. Only four habitations lay on the American side of the river: Ponce's, Stephenson's, and Magoffin's ranches and Hart's Mill. Because it was closest to El Paso, Van Horne selected Ponce's Ranch for the new post.

Except for the flagstaff, little served to mark the flat-roofed adobe buildings of Ponce's Ranch as a U.S. military installation. It lasted but two years anyway, for the commander in Santa Fe, who now had jurisdiction, decreed that his troops must be moved away from the towns. Towns, he reasoned, corrupted the soldiers and kept them from their proper occupation—chasing Indians out on the frontier. In September 1851, therefore, the garrison marched away from the Post Opposite El Paso and took station at Fort Fillmore, about thirty miles upriver.

But a need still existed at El Paso, as Inspector General J. K. F. Mansfield recognized during a tour of New Mexico forts in 1853. At his urging, the troops came back early in 1854 and established Fort Bliss, named in honor of a Mexican War veteran of distinction who had recently died. The new post was fixed not at Ponce's Ranch (now called Smith's Ranch) but a short distance downstream at Magoffin's Ranch, also known as Magoffinsville.

Throughout the rest of the 1850s, the men of Fort Bliss justified Mansfield's judgment. They campaigned tirelessly against the Mescalero Apaches in the Guadalupe and Sacramento mountains to the northeast and the Gila and Mogollon Apaches in the mountains to the northwest. They participated in Colonel Benjamin L. E. Bonneville's bruising campaign of 1857, which ended in the Battle of the Gila far to the west, in what later became Arizona. They even fought the Navajos in 1859.

Among the most active officers in 1855 were Captain James Longstreet and his lieutenant, George E. Pickett. Longstreet was married to the daughter of the department commander, General John Garland, and in 1858, perhaps not unrelatedly, succeeded in winning a choice staff assignment with the Pay Department. Scarcely five years later, Confederate General Longstreet would command the right of Lee's line at Gettysburg and launch one of his division commanders, General Pickett, in a charge destined to reverberate through history.

Except for a red sandy desert that supported almost nothing but mesquite, Fort Bliss at Magoffinsville was a pleasant post. An officer's wife remembered it as "the

OFFICERS' QUARTERS, CONCORDIA LOCATION, FORT BLISS

The problem with this location was that when it was dry the wagon wheels broke in the huge cracks in the parched clay and when it rained the post became a muddy bog impossible to get around in. Life was not too pleasant here, and the fort was soon moved.

59

most delightful station" her family ever had. Adobe barracks and quarters fronted on a tree-shaded parade ground. The Rio Grande flowed close by. The village of Franklin provided civilian amenities, while across the river Paso del Norte invited all with a variety of pleasures. As an officer recorded in 1856, "life at the post was dull enough until the fiestas commenced, then bull fights and billiards, bailes and monte, intrigues and crimes, made gay and noisy scenes where but an hour before all was as monotonous as the desert."

The Civil War interrupted this phase of Fort Bliss' history. Evacuated by regulars in 1861, it served as assembly point and base for Confederate General Henry H. Sibley's invasion of New Mexico in 1862. After the failure of that enterprise, the Texan troops burned the fort and withdrew. Federal detachments occupied Franklin and Hart's Mill for the balance of the war, but not until 1865 did regulars seek to rebuild the old post at Magoffinsville. It was a hopeless undertaking, for increasingly the river ate away at the buildings and corrals and threatened to carry away the entire fort. Finally, in 1868, the Army gave up on Magoffinsville.

The new site occupied slightly higher ground a mile down the river to the northeast, at the old Stephenson Ranch of Van Horne's time, now called Concordia Ranch. Here the troops built another adobe post on the usual pattern around a spacious rectangular parade ground. Like its predecessor, it relied on the nearby river for its water needs. There was a pond in an old river bed, but, as the surgeon noted, it was simply a "muddy nuisance." For a year this fort bore the name Camp Concordia, but in 1869 the Secretary of War restored the old designation. For almost a decade Fort Bliss at Concordia drowsed in the desert sun, a one-company post serving mainly to quarter troops who, as always, took delight in the attractions of the Mexican city across the river. Finally, in 1877, the War Department once more closed down Fort Bliss.

No sooner had the troops departed than violence erupted in the so-called "El Paso Salt War," which arose from a misguided attempt to impose taxes on salt deposits that had never been taxed. Even Texas Rangers could not restore order, and back came the Army. The abandoned buildings of Fort Bliss had already fallen into ruin, and for two years the troops were quartered in the city. In 1879, the War Department having decided they should stay, Fort Bliss found its way to still another location. At Hart's Mill, upstream at the mouth of the Pass of the North, the Army acquired 135 acres of land and commenced construction of another fort much like the earlier ones. For the first time the government had bought a site rather than, as previously, leased from private owners. Presumably Fort Bliss had finally put down lasting roots. But military needs soon collided with the vigorous growth of the city, now called El Paso instead of Franklin, and by 1890 the Army once again sought a new site.

Five miles northeast of the city, on the edge of La Noria Mesa, the Army bought a thousand acres of land and in October 1893 moved into a handsome new Fort Bliss that at last had found an enduring resting place. Appropriately, the first commander at the new site was Colonel Henry Lazelle, who as a lieutenant had campaigned out of Bliss against Apaches in the 1850s and had served with the contingent that abandoned it to the Confederates in 1861. As a permanent post with a long future, Fort Bliss on La Noria Mesa now shed all the disabilities of the typical frontier station and over the years evolved into a large, attractive, and comfortable billet.

Fort Bliss played a crucial role in the Mexican border disturbances of 1913–1917. Increasingly the border felt the shock waves of the shifting political allegiances of Mexican leaders and the revolutionary outbreaks that resulted. Troops in unprecedented numbers concentrated at Fort Bliss. For the first time, in 1915, a general officer commanded—Brigadier General John J. Pershing. In March 1916 trouble spilled across the boundary when Pancho

Villa and his followers charged into Columbus, New Mexico, and sacked the town. Within two days, with a formidable army, Pershing plunged into Mexico. Airplanes and motorized vehicles gave notice that the campaigns of Indian times had yielded to new dimensions of technology. Whole National Guard divisions mobilized at Fort Bliss for backup in case Pershing's invasion provoked war. It did not; in fact it ended rather ingloriously when the U.S. Army found Villa harder to catch than Apaches and settled for a face-saving diplomatic resolution of the matter. Throughout World War I, however, the cavalry, working out of Fort Bliss and other stations, patrolled the Mexican frontier while the doughboys fought in France.

Unthreatened by the extinction that overtook most other relics of the Indian frontier, Fort Bliss endured through the 1920s and 1930s as a major center for cavalry and artillery. Aviation and medical facilities were erected in 1920 and took on ever-increasing importance. Fort Bliss played its part in World War II and then in the postwar decades found a new mission that gave it a new lease on life: missiles. With a million-acre reservation, almost four thousand buildings, and twenty thousand soldiers, Fort Bliss had come far since its origins in a battalion of infantry quartered at Ponce's Ranch in 1849. But amid all the sophisticated weaponry of modern warfare, Fort Bliss yet today recalls these origins and the history and traditions to which they gave rise.

SOURCES: Billings, *Report on Barracks* and *Report on Hygiene*; Clendenen, *Blood on the Border*; Frazer, *Forts of the West*; Prucha, *Guide*.

PARADE GROUND, HART'S MILL LOCATION, FORT BLISS

This was an ideal location, and permanent buildings were constructed. Then the railroad insisted that the best location for its tracks was down the middle of the parade ground. Scheduling drills and marches around train schedules became too much of a headache, and the location was finally abandoned.

COMMANDING OFFICER'S QUARTERS, FORT BLISS

This building is commonly called Pershing House after its most famous occupant. General Pershing lived here with his only surviving son after a fire in California claimed the lives of his wife and other two children.

SUGGESTED READING

Billings, John S. *Report on Barracks and Hospitals, with Descriptions of Military Posts*. War Department, Surgeon General's Office, Circular No. 4. Washington, D.C., 1870.

—————. *Report on Hygiene of the United States Army, with Descriptions of Military Posts*. War Department, Surgeon General's Office, Circular No. 8. Washington, D.C., 1875.

Carter, Robert G. *On the Border with Mackenzie, or Winning West Texas from the Comanches*. New York: Antiquarian Press, 1961.

Clendenen, Clarence C. *Blood on the Border: The United States Army and the Mexican Irregulars*. New York: Macmillan, 1969.

Crimmins, Martin L. "The First Line of Army Posts Established in West Texas in 1849." *West Texas Historical Association Year Book*, vol. 19 (1943).

—————, ed. "Col. J. K. F. Mansfield's Report on the Inspection of the Department of Texas in 1856." 3 installments. *Southwestern Historical Quarterly*, vol. 42 (1938–1939).

—————, ed. "Freeman's Report on the Eighth Military Department [1853]." 13 installments. *Southwestern Historical Quarterly*, vols. 51 (1947–1948), 52 (1948–1949), 53 (1949–1950), and 54 (1950–1951).

Frazer, Robert W. *Forts of the West*. Norman: University of Oklahoma Press, 1965.

Green, Bill. *The Dancing Was Lively: Fort Concho, Texas, Social History, 1867 to 1882*. N.p., 1974.

Haley, J. Evetts. *Fort Concho and the Texas Frontier*. San Angelo, Tex., 1952.

Holden, William C. "Frontier Defense [in Texas], 1846–1860." *West Texas Historical Association Year Book*, vol. 6 (1930).

—————. "Frontier Defense in Texas during the Civil War." *West Texas Historical Association Year Book*, vol. 4 (1928).

Leckie, William F. *The Buffalo Soldiers: A Narrative of Negro Cavalry in the West*. Norman: University of Oklahoma Press, 1967.

McConnell, H. H. *Five Years a Cavalryman, or Sketches of Regular Army Life on the Texas Frontier*. Jacksboro, Tex., 1889.

Maury, Dabney H. *Recollections of a Virginian in the Mexican, Indian and Civil Wars*. New York: Charles Scribner's Sons, 1894.

Prucha, Francis Paul. *Guide to the Military Posts of the United States*. Madison: State Historical Society of Wisconsin, 1964.

Richardson, Rupert N. *The Comanche Barrier to South Plains Settlement*. Glendale, Calif.: Arthur H. Clark Co., 1933.

—————. *The Frontier of Northwest Texas, 1846 to 1876*. Glendale, Calif.: Arthur H. Clark Co., 1963.

Rister, Carl C. *Fort Griffin on the Texas Frontier*. Norman: University of Oklahoma Press, 1956.

Scobee, Barry. *Old Fort Davis*. San Antonio: Naylor, 1947.

Stallard, Patricia Y. *Glittering Misery: Dependents of the Indian Fighting Army*. Fort Collins, Colo.: Old Army Press, 1978.

Utley, Robert M. *Frontier Regulars: The United States Army and the Indian, 1866–1891*. New York: Macmillan, 1973.

—————. *Frontiersmen in Blue: The United States Army and the Indian, 1848–1865*. New York: Macmillan, 1967.

Viele, Mrs. Egbert L. *Following the Drum: A Glimpse of Frontier Life*. New York, 1958. Reprint, with introduction by Sandra Myres, Lincoln: University of Nebraska Press, 1984.

Wallace, Ernest. *Ranald S. Mackenzie on the Texas Frontier*. Lubbock: West Texas Museum Association, 1965.

Webb, Walter Prescott. *The Texas Rangers: A Century of Frontier Defense*. Boston: Houghton Mifflin, 1935.

Whisenhunt, Donald W. *Fort Richardson: Outpost on the Texas Frontier*. El Paso, Tex., 1968.

Winfrey, Dorman H., ed. *Texas Indian Papers, 1846–1859*. Austin: Texas State Library, 1960.

—————, with James M. Day. *Texas Indian Papers, 1860–1916*. Austin: Texas State Library, 1961.

IF THESE WALLS COULD SPEAK ★ HISTORIC FORTS OF TEXAS